PRAISE FOR
YOUR TE

"A team that reaches its full capacity is a force to be reckoned with! Robert Glazer provides an evidence-based road map for achieving this goal."

—Cal Newport, New York Times Bestselling Author
of *A World Without Email* and *Deep Work*

"As a leader in a disruptive industry, it's often a tough balance to manage and grow your team at the same speed and scale as what the organization requires. *Elevate Your Team* is a great framework for leaders who are growing their teams in an ever-changing, quick-paced environment to meet the needs for today while building the capabilities and workforce needed for tomorrow."

—Aicha Evans, CEO of Zoox

"Business leadership isn't just about building companies—it's about 'Working Together' to create value for all of the stakeholders and the greater good. With *Elevate Your Team*, Glazer shares an innovative approach that will help your people level up and 'Work Together' to become the leaders that the organization will need tomorrow."

—Alan Mulally, Former President and CEO of the Ford Motor
Company & Former CEO of Boeing Commercial Airplanes

"*Elevate Your Team* is a new way to think about culture and talent development. Learn how to play the long-game with your company culture and discover actionable steps to build your team's capacity, help your people reach their full potential, and train the future leaders of your organization."

—Dorie Clark, *Wall Street Journal* Bestselling Author of *The Long Game* and Executive Education Faculty, Duke University Fuqua School of Business

"*Elevate Your Team* isn't the same old tired management playbook you've read many times before—it's a new perspective on business leadership and talent development. Glazer shares how to build the team's capacity holistically, help people reach their full potential, and develop the organization's next generation of leaders."

—JeVon McCormick, President, and CEO of Scribe Media, Bestselling Author of *Modern Leader*

"Any leader can do $10,000/hour work by building and leading a highly effective team. *Elevate Your Team* won't just help you improve as a leader and scale your team; it will also help you create a self-reinforcing flywheel within your organization by giving you the tools you need to train and nurture the next generation of leaders at your organization."

—Khe Hy, "Oprah For Millennials" and Founder of Rad Reads

ELEVATE

YOUR TEAM

*Empower Your Team to Reach
Their Full Potential and Build
a Business that Builds Leaders*

ROBERT GLAZER

simple **truths**
▶ Small books. BIG IMPACT.

To everyone in my own life who pushed me to
grow my capacity and reach my potential

Copyright © 2023 by Robert Glazer & Kendall Marketing Group, LLC
Cover and internal design © 2023 by Sourcebooks
Cover design by Jackie Cummings
Internal design by Ashley Holstrom/Sourcebooks

Sourcebooks, Simple Truths, and the colophon are
registered trademarks of Sourcebooks.

This publication is designed to provide accurate and authoritative information
in regard to the subject matter covered. It is sold with the understanding
that the publisher is not engaged in rendering legal, accounting, or other
professional service. If legal advice or other expert assistance is required,
the services of a competent professional person should be sought. —*From
a Declaration of Principles Jointly Adopted by a Committee of the American
Bar Association and a Committee of Publishers and Associations*

Published by Simple Truths, an imprint of Sourcebooks
P.O. Box 4410, Naperville, Illinois 60567-4410
(630) 961-3900
sourcebooks.com

Cataloging-in-Publication Data is on file with the Library of Congress.

Printed and bound in the United States of America.
VP 10 9 8 7 6 5 4 3 2 1

TABLE OF CONTENTS

INTRODUCTION

I couldn't decide if I was a genius or an idiot.

It was 2017, and the company I founded, Acceleration Partners (AP), had just completed another year of double-digit growth. We had also recently won three consecutive *Inc.* 500 awards from 2013 to 2015, an honor bestowed each year to the five hundred fastest-growing private companies in America.

From the outside, we were on a fast track, but the view from inside the company told a different story.

Even though we had a healthy company culture and had even won a few Best Places to Work awards, we had an emerging talent development problem that threatened to jeopardize our growth and our culture.

The problem wasn't a fundamental failure to develop our

people. In fact, several of our hires from the early years of AP were keeping pace with our growth and would go on to take important executive leadership roles.

However, there was an increasingly large group of employees who struggled to keep pace. While they improved each year, they weren't growing as fast as the company. Despite their progress, these employees still fell behind and often hit a wall at the worst possible time.

For a made-up example of our challenge (for obvious legal and ethical reasons), imagine we hired a Marketing Manager to oversee our marketing portfolio. While the manager improved in their first year at the company, within a year or two, AP grew so quickly that we found ourselves needing director-level work on our marketing team: a leader who could build and manage a team of marketers rather than just an individual contributor who could execute marketing projects. To be fair, we needed both roles.

In situations like this one—and we had several—we had a choice to make with a relatively new manager who was talented but objectively not ready to step up to the director level and lead a team. This type of scenario presents a few options that don't feel so great:

1. Hire a director above them, wounding their pride in the process.

2. Transition them out of the company, and replace them with a director.

3. Promote them into a director role they aren't ready for, hope for the best, and then try to find a new manager.

The first choice is logical but often turns a high performer into an unengaged employee; they believe leadership doesn't trust them to step up, and they feel disappointed going from being in charge to having someone else take over.

The second choice is efficient, but it diminishes trust throughout the company when people start to believe they'll be replaced whenever your business takes a leap forward. Plus, you lose a good manager who knows how to deliver marketing outcomes for the company, creating at least a temporary setback.

The third choice is the path companies usually take, especially with people who have performed well up to that point. Promoting from within is cheaper and faster than hiring someone new, and it boosts a business's reputation on the recruiting and retention fronts. But while this route can often yield a surprise overperformer, it can also create poor outcomes for both the employee and the company, especially if the newly promoted director finds themselves in over their head and their team suffers as a result.

We found ourselves facing these types of decisions regularly.

Our employees were improving, just not quite fast enough, and we didn't have a clear strategy to address that challenge. If you're a leader of a team, department, or organization with this type of high-growth trajectory, you've probably experienced this same conundrum.

In the moment, I was stumped. But looking back, I see so clearly that I possessed the answer to this exact problem. I just had not yet been able to connect the dots.

During the same year we were facing these challenges, I had hit a similar roadblock personally. I was struggling to get any publisher interest in my second book. Tentatively titled *Friday Forward*, the book was a selection of fifty-two short stories from my weekly newsletter of the same name, which had grown from a weekly note sent to my team of forty to a global audience of nearly one hundred thousand readers worldwide. Even though I knew the content of the messages resonated with so many people each week, every publisher gave me the same feedback: they weren't excited about a compilation.

I'm not quick to give up, but I was nearly ready to accept that the timing for the book just wasn't right. But then my literary agent gave me a challenge that changed everything: rather than pitching a compilation of the best stories from the newsletter, he pushed me to pull the key themes and ideas from those stories and attempt to shape them into a concept for a book.

After all I'd invested in building an audience for *Friday Forward*, I figured it was worth a shot.

After nearly a year of digging through newsletters and developing a cohesive framework based on the lessons of those stories and lots of discussions, I arrived at the capacity building framework that served as the basis for my eventual second book: *Elevate*.

In *Elevate*, I defined "capacity building" as the method through which individuals seek, acquire, and develop the skills and abilities to consistently perform at a higher level in pursuit of their innate potential. That book was entirely focused on individual capacity building across personal and professional life in four key areas—spiritual, intellectual, physical, and emotional. One of the core principles of capacity building is the idea that each of us is the same person at work and outside it, and lasting achievement in one of those spheres is dependent on growth in the other.

The principles, tactics, and tools I articulated in *Elevate* were the same things I'd done to level up as a leader for years to that point and had started to share with our emerging leaders. But it was only once I finished my first draft of *Elevate* and had the capacity building framework laid out clearly that I had my idiot-genius epiphany: I had spent years cultivating all these ideas for individual growth and performance, but I failed to realize those same ideas could form the backbone of our employee development strategy.

I realized the same capacity building framework for individuals could serve as a foundation for a blueprint to help our employees meet the challenges of growth. To some degree, we were already using the principle of holistic growth as a guidepost for our training process:

▸ As part of our management training, we had started helping new managers identify and articulate their personal core values.

▸ We used our fully remote model to give employees flexibility to structure their workdays around their personal passions, whether that was pursuing a performing art, training for high-level athletic performance, or even just being more present with their families.

▸ We had even piloted an initiative we called our "Dream Program" where we helped several employees pursue or achieve a highly fulfilling personal goal. These aspirations ranged from training for marathons, to traveling to Greece to visit distant relatives, to even tracking down a long-lost sibling.

Sometimes in life, we find ourselves unintentionally running in the perfect direction. It occurred to me that through the programs listed above and other initiatives, we were already dabbling in capacity building, helping our people grow outside work and reaping the benefits during the workday as a result.

Then it hit me: the key to accelerating employee's growth trajectory was doubling down and making this unintentional capacity building strategy more deliberate and company-wide.

Today, we are focused most on helping our people grow holistically. Capacity building is a core part of our culture, aligned with one of our three core values, "Excel and Improve." It is the centerpiece of our leadership training, which focuses as heavily on building self-awareness, authenticity, and individual ability as a leader as it does on management tactics such as running a meeting, giving feedback, or delegating.

The results speak for themselves. Even though we've grown our top-line revenue by 4,000 percent in the past decade and grown from 7 to over 300 employees, we've kept an employee turnover rate that is historically far below our industry average and have won over twenty-five Best Places to Work awards. Many of the people who have left our organization, our AP alumni, have taken on leadership roles at other companies, which is a great outcome and something we support.

This is the playbook for a talent development strategy that will build your business by building your people. It will show you how to help your employees get better holistically in four key areas that elevate professional and personal performance: spiritual, intellectual, physical, and emotional capacity. In the process, you'll be creating an ultimate win-win for your company and your employees—you'll help your people reach their career goals, and you'll build a team of high performers who help hit your organizational goals and eventually can step into leadership roles. If you're a leader at any level in a high-growth organization, you've probably experienced the types of pain points described earlier. You might be hoping to become the type of organization that promotes from within for the majority of your leadership roles. The key to doing this is to train your employees not just to excel at the job you've hired them to do today but to help them grow to take on the roles of tomorrow.

By the time you're through with this book, you'll have a clear understanding of how to implement this strategy and framework throughout your organization and a wealth of tactics you can put into action. If you find your team's growth stagnating, the key to kick-starting improvement will likely be found in one or more of the four capacities outlined in the chapters ahead.

To be clear, this is not an academic book you'd likely find on a business school syllabus. Instead of theories and studies that stem from controlled experiments run by people who are not growing and leading teams day to day, this book shares the proven strategies that built our organization and the organizations we've exchanged best practices with over the years.

In short, my goal is to teach you how to do something very similar to what we did: to build a business that builds people—both professionally and personally.

Elevate was eventually published in 2019 and became a *Wall Street Journal* bestseller, two years after every publisher turned me away. That same year, AP hit a major milestone: $20 million in revenue, with nearly 170 employees. As I write this, we have over 300 employees, and we've built our leadership team by promoting 80 percent of our leaders from within.

By doubling down on capacity building, we've beaten the talent development challenge we faced just a few years ago, and we have the right playbook to avoid repeating the same cycle as we grow from here.

I think you'll be amazed at the results you'll get from building your team's capacity and will find it the most rewarding way to build and grow a business. And you also might be surprised to learn this whole journey started with a simple illustration on a fogged-up shower door—more on that in a minute.

Chapter One

WHY YOU NEED CAPACITY BUILDING

"Knowledge is different from all other resources.
It makes itself constantly obsolete, so that today's
advanced knowledge is tomorrow's ignorance."

—Peter Drucker

No matter where you work or what industry you're in, I bet I can describe a top performer at your company:

► They have a strong understanding of their strengths and weaknesses. Just as importantly, they know how to emphasize their strengths while minimizing their weaknesses.

- They have a clear direction for their career that is aligned with their personal values.
- They are a voracious learner and a disciplined executor.
- Rather than being satisfied with a high level of performance, they consistently seek out feedback to help them learn and improve.
- They have developed an intentional structure to their day with positive habits.
- They have good physical and mental discipline. They make thoughtful decisions about how they use their time and energy and work smarter, not harder. They may even have a regular morning routine and a consistent exercise time that is blocked off in their daily schedule.
- They connect well with others, are unafraid to be vulnerable in the right moments, and take ownership of their actions and situations rather than blaming others.

If your organization doesn't have someone who fits this profile, know that your competitors do—especially the ones that are leading your industry.

But if you don't have these types of people at your organization or on your team today, not all is lost. The qualities described above are not innate to an individual or an organization. They can be developed through intentionality, training, and commitment.

I know this from experience. Like many important learnings in life, this story starts with a shower epiphany. At the time, I was contemplating a question that had nagged me for months about our own business: *Why do some people manage to keep up with, or exceed, Acceleration Partners' high rate of growth while others are consumed by it?*

Suddenly, the answer hit me. I turned off the water, jumped out of the shower, and ran to my desk, determined not to forget the image that I had just traced out on the fogged-up glass of the shower door.

Water dripped onto the page, running through to the cherrywood of my desk and smudging my work as I sketched a diagram that would go on to change the trajectory of our business.

At that time, AP had been growing at an annual rate of over 30 percent for several years; in effect, the company was doubling in size approximately every two and half years. And while this growth was exciting in one respect, it also caused a lot of growing pains, especially with our people. Even though we had a robust training program and an award-winning workplace culture, too many of our employees were falling off the bus as we picked up speed.

What I found most frustrating was that I did not have a way to predict which employees could keep up with and even thrive during the company's growth and which ones would be trampled by it. It wasn't as simple as seeing high performers continue to excel while lower performers kept struggling. In fact, we had cases where an early top performer went on to fizzle while other employees who did not necessarily stand out when they first joined the company improved their performance over time and rose to take on more demanding roles. Some of those late bloomers even ended up in key leadership positions at the company.

This made no sense to me and seemed to defy many of the lessons I had learned over the years from some of the best minds in leadership and management. My understanding was that A-Players don't usually turn into B-Players over time, and B-Players rarely turn into A-Players. But the evidence was pretty clear that these rules of thumb did not always apply at AP. I really needed to understand why.

The breakthrough I had in the shower that day was that an employee's growth trajectory had nothing to do with their experience or even their performance in their current role. Instead, the most important predictor of future performance was an employee's ability to improve at a high rate, irrespective of their starting point.

I was visualizing our company's annual growth rate as a line on a graph. Then I thought about people who either rose above or fell below that growth line as it advanced upward. That visualization of our employees' growth relative to our company growth is what I frantically sketched when I stepped out the shower.

After reflecting for a few more days, I created a few more lines, figured out the right label for each one, and suddenly had a clear concept that I could share with my team to explain what we had been experiencing throughout our rapid growth.

In fast-growing organizations, the difference between people who can ride the growth wave and those who get consumed by it is their ability to increase their capacity at a rate that equals or exceeds the company's growth rate. Just because someone is great at their job today doesn't mean they will be ready for the job of tomorrow, which is why some A-Players struggle as their roles evolve. In contrast, some employees who did not stand out initially actually improve as they are given more responsibility. They might not start as an A-Player, but they find a way to grow and develop into a significant asset to the organization over time.

Most leaders of fast-growing organizations are familiar with the concept of the valley of death. This is the phenomenon where a period of high growth is followed by a downturn or a period of stagnation. Many companies don't survive these valleys of death, while others only make it out battered and bruised and after significant turnover.

I didn't realize it at the time, but we were in one of these valleys of death when I had my shower epiphany. Many of our early stars were fizzling out, and it wasn't easy to identify who could step up and who would stumble along the way.

This problem isn't rare or unique. Many high-growth organizations struggle to keep their teams together through periods of rapid growth. In fact, I received the same piece of wisdom from several different coaches and peers who had followed the same growth trajectory AP was on: *Every time you double your company's size, you will break 50 percent of your processes and 50 percent of your people.*

Unfortunately, the way many companies address this challenge is to follow the churn-and-burn playbook of Silicon Valley—hire young employees, work them hard, burn them out, and swap them out for a new crop who are eager to take their seats on the roller coaster.

This 50 percent rule was pretty prescient. Even though we weren't losing half our people every time we doubled, we were still experiencing significant disruption with each leap forward. This was not how we wanted to build a business; we did not want to be a race car that had to change its tires every few laps around the track. We wanted to grow AP by growing with our people and bringing them along for the ride—a mutually beneficial outcome where our team members lifted each other and the organization up as they improved.

We needed a different strategy. What we really wanted was to build a culture that helped build better people.

Visualizing the Capacity Building Road Map

The core of my shower epiphany was that we couldn't think of employee performance or ability as static. Rather, we should think about how an employee's development trajectory relates to the company's growth curve. Here is a refined version of the chart I drew and shared with the company a few weeks later, with the four groups that comprised most of our employees identified on the learning curve:

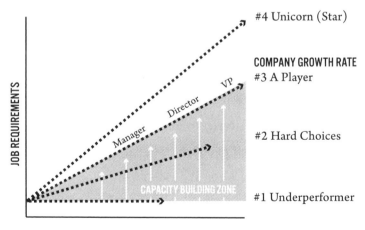

The axes measure the role requirement for a given employee across the time span of company growth. The graph represents how someone performs in their role as the expectations of that role increase over time. Generally speaking, most employees within an organization fall into one of four groups. Some are Underperformers, while others are A-Players or Unicorns. The rest fall somewhere in the Capacity Building Zone (CBZ).

The solid line in the graph represents the growth rate of the company and the most senior role for a given business function at a given point of growth. Let's use marketing as an example. Early on in a company's growth trajectory, the firm's most senior marketing person may be a manager. However, once the company grows a few years down the line, the company likely needs a full marketing team, possibly run by a VP who oversees directors and managers working below them.

As these more senior roles are added, every business must determine whether to promote from within or hire from outside the company. It's easier to make this decision if leadership understands how their people fit into each of the categories in the chart above. Here is how it breaks down:

▸ **Underperformers:** These are the people who start at the company's baseline of performance but don't have the ability or desire to improve over time. As the company grows and an employee's role demands new and different skills, this underperformance becomes more glaring. Soon enough, it becomes clear that an Underperformer just isn't getting the job done, and it's time to exit them from their organization.

▸ **Unicorns (Stars):** A Unicorn is the highest-level performer you can have at an organization. These are the rare employees who grow even faster than the company requires. When you hire a Unicorn as a manager, they deliver director-level work before your expected promotion timetable and can continue as the leader of their given function. When you do promote them, they continue to set the new standard. A company may only have one or two of these Unicorns at any given time, and it's up to leadership to do whatever it takes to keep them happy—be sure to pay them well and load them up with equity.

▸ **A-Players:** An A-Player is not an absolute label that describes a particular person. Instead, an A-Player is the right person in the right role at the right time. Someone can rise to an A-Player level, and they can fall out of that tier. A consistent A-Player grows at the exact rate that the company grows and can be promoted to higher levels of the organization in a leadership capacity as the company requires those roles.

For example, a startup might hire someone to serve as their HR Manager. As the company grows and requires a Director of HR rather than just a manager, that person has built the capacity to elevate into that director seat. Then, when the company grows further and suddenly needs a VP of HR or even a Chief HR Officer, the A-Player is ready to take on that role as well. Whatever the company demands as it grows, a consistent A-Player is ready to fill that role—because they are growing at the same rate, they are always the right person in the right seat at the right time.

▸ **The Capacity Building Zone (CBZ):** The majority of employees in a growth company will fall into this category. These are the people who are below the company growth line at a given moment. While most employees in the CBZ are dedicated to improving, not everyone can build their capacity up to match the organization's growth line. And when it comes time to make a tough call, it is the employees in this group that will keep managers and leaders awake at night.

Employees who can't climb to the top of the CBZ aren't necessarily poor performers. They may be improving dramatically each year and earning promotions, but their individual rate of improvement is still below the company's growth line. For example, getting 20 percent better each year is typically a huge achievement, but in a company or team that grows 40 percent each year, it's usually not enough to stay in the most senior role within their given function. In especially fast-growing companies, most people fall into the CBZ because it's really hard to get that much better each year. For example, it's very unlikely for even the best employee to grow from a bookkeeper into a CFO in a few years, but if a company is growing 200 percent per year, the role needed for the leader of the finance department will move from a bookkeeper to a controller to a CFO quickly.

While many of the principles in this book will apply to employees who are in the CBZ, the same principles extend to your A-Players and Unicorns, who often have the most upside. The coming chapters are a guide to how you can build your people's capacity—across the organization—at the same rate that the company is growing. It's easier to build a scalable business when your people can grow with the company and take key leadership roles as they become available.

Leaders can use capacity building as a cornerstone strategy to achieve more growth with less turnover, give their most talented people a reason to stay, and build a culture where improvement is incentivized and contagious. Let's talk about how.

How Capacity Building Works

Capacity building is a framework to build a team that grows with your business rather than ending up with a team that is trampled by your business's growth. This book goes into detail on how to leverage each of the four capacities to elevate your team's performance and describes actionable ways to help your team grow in all four key areas.

As I first defined in my previous book, *Elevate*, capacity building is the method through which individuals seek, acquire, and develop the skills and abilities to consistently perform at a higher level in pursuit of their innate potential.

Remember earlier when I described your perfect employee? Here's how I knew—capacity building in an organization gives employees what they need to excel in four areas:

▸ **Spiritual Capacity:** Understanding who you are, what you want most, and the standards you live by. People with high spiritual capacity have a clear understanding of their purpose in life, the nonnegotiable core values that guide their most important decisions, and their strengths and weaknesses in their personal and professional lives.

▸ **Intellectual Capacity:** How you think, learn, plan, and execute with discipline. People with high intellectual capacity are the ones who seem to get more done in less time—they set clear goals for themselves, build the skills necessary to achieve those goals, learn constantly, and develop the habits they need to stay on track.

▶ **Physical Capacity:** Your health, well-being, and physical performance. People with high physical capacity have built the resilience and stamina needed to excel in stressful or challenging situations. They manage their energy and avoid burning out by working smarter, not harder.

▶ **Emotional Capacity:** How you react to challenging situations, your emotional mindset, and the quality of your relationships. People with high emotional capacity always bring good perspective to challenging situations. When others are panicked by high stakes or frustrated by setbacks, people with high emotional capacity are calmly navigating challenges, learning from failures, and rallying the troops. They work well with others and command respect from direct reports, colleagues, and leadership alike.

You'll notice that these four core competencies greatly affect both personal and professional spheres of life. This is not a coincidence. The fact is that we are not different people at work and in our personal lives. This has always been the case but is becoming truer as many companies encourage employees to bring their whole selves to work. What we do outside work affects our professional performance. Consider the following:

- A person who struggles with time management, prioritization, and punctuality at work probably has the same issues in their personal life.

- A person who has low energy or little regard for their well-being outside work probably isn't showing up to work with a ton of energy.

- A person who is unhappy, unfulfilled, or frustrated with their personal life will often see some of those challenges spill into their work performance, and vice versa.

Plus, employees increasingly want their employers to value them as people, not just as interchangeable cogs in a machine. They want to have a chance to advance in their careers. They want to feel successful in their roles and to have some autonomy over their work. They want to be able to create space in their lives for their personal passions and fulfillment, even if they know there isn't always a perfect fifty-fifty balance between work and life. They want work to be an integrated part of life, not exist only outside it.

Capacity building helps your employees achieve these things. It gives them a framework to gain the understanding of what they want most in life and the discipline to go get it. It helps them build better habits and routines in their day that allow them to better use their time and save energy by avoiding unimportant things. It empowers them to build relationships that make them stronger rather than draining their energy.

This investment yields a higher level of personal and professional achievement, which fuels better job performance, which drives company growth, which allows leaders to reinvest more into their people. It's a virtuous cycle that helps everyone grow and inspire others within their personal and professional circles to do the same.

There aren't many true win-wins in life and business, but helping your team get more out of life as they simultaneously contribute more to your business is one of them.

If you commit yourself and your organization to capacity building, not only will you unlock a better level of performance on your team, but you will also see changes and improvement far beyond your organization's walls. In the next four chapters, you'll see specific strategies and tactics designed to help your team build their capacity in the four areas listed above.

But first, you need to understand two core principles needed to make capacity building a part of your cultural DNA. One pertains to personal leadership, and the other relates to organizational leadership.

Capacity Building Starts With You

Let's be honest. You can't effectively motivate and inspire others unless you are leading as your authentic self.

This is especially true with capacity building. Whether you lead a small team, a department, or an organization—or are aspiring to lead in the future—the first step to leading a team that constantly builds capacity is to build your own capacity as a leader. To do this, it is helpful to ask yourself a few questions:

▶ **Spiritual Capacity:** Are you clear about what you value most and your strengths? Do you use that knowledge to lead authentically?

▶ **Intellectual Capacity:** Are you consistently able to learn, grow, and accomplish what you want to do each day, or do you often find yourself struggling to start, falling off course, or lacking discipline?

▶ **Physical Capacity:** Do you feel like you effectively manage your energy, or are you constantly sleep-deprived, stressed out, and burned out?

▶ **Emotional Capacity:** Do you surround yourself with people who encourage you, value you, and help you learn, or do you have a lot of close friends and family who leave you feeling exhausted after each interaction? Are you willing to be vulnerable? Are you good at differentiating between what you can and can't control and spending your time with the former?

For more questions like this—and a sense of where you can improve most in your capacity building journey, check out my Four Capacities Quiz.

Your answers to these questions provide a sense of where you stand in your own capacity building journey. Right now, you're either confident in your responses or you're realizing you still have one or more areas where you need to grow.

You don't have to master capacity building to adopt it as a philosophy for your team, but people often react more to what you do than what you say. You'll be a much more effective coach if capacity building is visible in the way you show up each day and if you can point to examples of how you've used it in your own life.

Making Capacity Building an Organizational Priority

Since I first published *Elevate*, I have spoken with many organizations and groups about how to use capacity building as a personal and leadership development framework. I have seen many individuals use the four capacities to elevate their personal performance and then teach the same concepts to their teams.

But this individualized strategy alone won't transform an organization. To really change your team and help your people reach their full potential—and help your business grow as well—you need to invest company time and resources in capacity building and commit to growing your team in these four areas.

You can't just preach to your people about growth and improvement. You have to develop a culture that encourages and rewards it. Instead of focusing leadership and management training solely on job-related skills and tactics, help your up-and-coming leaders build their capacity with the strategies shared throughout this book.

Capacity building requires organizations to invest in their people holistically. It's not just about making your team better at work or maximizing their value to your organization today. It's also about helping them grow as people and viewing the benefits the organization receives as a primary by-product, not as the only output.

There's an old adage where a CFO and CEO are speaking,

and the CFO says, "What if we train our people and they leave?" to which the CEO replies, "What if we don't and they stay?"

In other words, you shouldn't be worrying that your employees will leave after you've invested so much in them. You should be more concerned if you don't have people on your bus who can take you to where you need to go.

Preparing for the Journey

One of the best hires we've ever made at AP came to us through a Craigslist ad for a copywriter. In 2011, Sarah Dayes had just made the difficult decision to shut down her retail business and was looking for freelance work. She saw our ad and joined our small team shortly thereafter.

Soon after we hired her, it became evident that Sarah had the capacity to do much more than just copywriting. Within a couple of years, she was leading our five-person digital strategy team, which was the smaller part of our business. Soon after, the head of our affiliate business, the largest part of our company, decided to move overseas, and we were wrestling with how to fill her role. Despite lacking any experience in the area, Sarah raised her hand.

Sarah's lack of experience initially made me hesitant, especially because affiliate marketing often takes people a long time to learn, let alone master. But what Sarah lacked in credentials, she made up for in capacity building ability—she was fearless and a fast learner who was always open to feedback and up for a challenge. We decided to elevate her into the role.

It was a better decision than we ever could have imagined. Today, Sarah is AP's Chief Customer Officer, overseeing a global team of over two hundred people. She is also one of our best success stories of capacity building in our organization.

Elevating your team through capacity building isn't easy, but the rewards are immense. Your people will need you to support and mentor them and give them honest, fair feedback when they fall short of certain deliverables and goals. They will need you to help them grow beyond their professional sphere and make changes in their own lives beyond the workplace. As you'll see in the next chapter, they'll even need you to help them gain clarity on the most important principles in their lives.

If it sounds difficult, that's because it is. But it's worth the work, and my hope is the chapters ahead can provide both the tools and the confidence you need to make it a reality in your organization.

Chapter Two

BUILD YOUR TEAM'S SPIRITUAL CAPACITY

"The two most important days in your life are the day you are born and the day you find out why."

—Author unknown

As Andrew stepped forward to share with the group, his voice trembled and it appeared as if he was holding back tears. Not only had he discovered one of his core values, but he had come to the shocking realization that what he expected most firmly from his team was something he had been lacking himself as a leader: self-awareness.

We were in the middle of a leadership training workshop, and I was guiding a group of up-and-coming managers through an exercise to identify their personal core values. The exercise challenged the attendees to think deeply on a series of personal questions: in what environments they are happiest, what qualities in others they find most challenging, and even what they'd want said about them in a eulogy.

In reflecting on the questions, Andrew (not his real name) realized that he was greatly impacted in childhood by a parent's lack of self-awareness. This parent, who Andrew loved deeply, was the type of person who could never quite read a room, could occasionally be a bit too loud, or would sometimes have one drink too many. Andrew realized that in large part due to this childhood experience, self-awareness had become one of his paramount personal core values.

This value came from personal pain but led to professional challenges as well, especially as a team leader. Andrew was a talented manager, but because of this third-rail value, when team members showed a lack of self-awareness, he often overreacted. Nothing set Andrew off more than when a team member talked too much on a client call, failed to listen to other people, or gave an unrealistic appraisal of their own abilities. Andrew knew these things frustrated him immensely as a manager, but before this moment, he had not been clear about why.

The exercise unlocked the answer for Andrew. He gained a deeper understanding of his own behavior and a vocabulary to communicate to his team just how important self-awareness was, leading to better outcomes for all.

Andrew's story points to one of the foundational truths of organizational capacity building: to become an authentic leader and work effectively with others, we first must first gain a clear understanding of ourselves. A leader who cannot articulate what is most important to them, doesn't understand their core values or drivers, and doesn't have a grasp of their strengths or weaknesses is unlikely to be very effective. Leadership is dependent on authenticity, and this is where spiritual capacity enters the equation.

While the term *spiritual* is often used in a religious context, it has a different meaning in capacity building. Spiritual capacity is about understanding who you are, what you want most, and the standards you live by. Teams and leaders with high spiritual capacity must have clear personal core values, self-awareness about their strengths and weaknesses, and alignment between those principles and the roles they hold within the team.

Building your team's spiritual capacity requires two key steps: As a leader, you must ensure that you have clarity on your own personal core values, strengths, and weaknesses. This is the only way to lead as your authentic self and communicate to your team which behaviors or traits are most important to you and why.

You then need to help your employees get clarity on who

they are at their core and empower them to develop their own authentic leadership style. When your people have this type of self-awareness, they will be more fulfilled in their personal lives, more engaged in their professional lives, and more effective at leading others. They may even realize there is something in their lives that is misaligned with their values, creating underlying dissatisfaction.

Every element of capacity building is crucial to individual or team success, but spiritual capacity has to come first, as it lays the foundation for the other three. You won't maximize your return on investment in the other capacities until you've built your spiritual capacity as a leader and helped your team do the same. A beautiful house built on an unsteady foundation may have great curb appeal but will eventually sink, crack, or crumble.

Investing in your team's spiritual capacity is a key reframing of leadership development. If you can help employees build their spiritual capacity *before* they step into leadership roles, they will be much better prepared for the task and more likely to grow into high-performing leaders who stay with your organization as it scales. Here's how to get started.

Starting With Values

Newly minted leaders tend to emulate practices and behaviors they've admired most about the managers they've had or do the opposite of the managerial tactics that frustrated them most.

I know this from personal experience, having recognized that my leadership style had become a patchwork quilt of the best practices of others, some of which did not feel right or authentic.

This form of emulation is a logical progression of trial and error for managers, but it's not a recipe for the highest level of leadership. This approach can leave you without a clear compass to navigate difficult situations or make tough choices. Few things feel worse as a leader than taking an important action and feeling like it's not authentic to you at your core. Likewise, few things make a team lose confidence in their leader faster than when the leader demonstrates a lack of conviction in their own words or actions.

This is where core values come in. Core values are the nonnegotiable principles that are most important to you. They are distinctly different from an organization's core values. Organizational core values, whether explicit or implicit, reflect the qualities or behaviors that the organization rewards. Personal core values provide guidance from within and reflect the qualities or behaviors that cause you to be engaged or disengaged.

While you don't need your work to reflect all your core values, all the time, there ultimately has to be alignment between what you do at work and what you believe most deeply.

Personal core values are the guideposts that keep you on track in life; consciously or unconsciously, they drive your most important decisions. Once you are clear about your core values, everything in your life makes a bit more sense, and your most important decisions are easier.

I say this from personal experience, as I was not an early adopter of personal core values. In fact, I was six years into running my own business before I gave them any deep thought.

But that all changed in 2013 when I attended a small, immersive leadership training program with Entrepreneurs' Organization. In those sessions, the facilitators emphasized the importance of authentic leadership, supported by the leader's personal core values. I left the training certain that I had very strong core values and determined to reach a point where I could articulate them clearly.

Naturally, I went looking for the how—a clear process for developing my own core values. To my surprise, I couldn't find a road map, so I spent a significant chunk of time figuring one out myself. Over six months, I spent several hours brainstorming, reflecting, and refining my list. After some trial and error, I settled on five values that summarize the nonnegotiable descriptors of who I am as a person and as a leader:

- Find A Better Way and Share It
- Self-Reliance
- Respectful Authenticity
- Long-Term Orientation
- Health and Vitality

Getting this clarity unlocked enormous improvements in my life. I was able to use my values to be more judicious with my time and energy, removing things from my life that didn't serve my principles. I was also able to use them to lead authentically as myself and to communicate what matters most to me to the people I lead. Almost all the highlights you'll read about in the About the Author section of this book—the company culture awards, the books, the speeches— came after this inflection point of defining my core values.

As a leader, if you don't have clarity on your core values, you will struggle to lead authentically. Here's an example.

One of my core values, as mentioned above, is to "Find A Better Way and Share It." As a result, I am not someone who likes to keep the status quo. I expect people on the teams I lead to strive to improve both the business and themselves. Some people excel under this type of leadership, and some people do not. It's crucial for the people I lead to know this about me up front. That clarity is extremely powerful and pays dividends for me, the people I lead, and our organization.

Core values are just as important to the personal sphere of life, if not more important. Without clear values, you may be navigating your life outside work without a GPS—while you might get to your destination eventually, you'll spend a lot of time and experience real pain running in the wrong direction.

Once I had clarity on my values and saw the benefits of that clarity, I became passionate about helping leaders on our team find their own values. I took the self-designed process that led me to my own core values and began to develop it into a teachable curriculum that we used in our advanced leadership training program described above.

Not only have we helped dozens of our leaders define their own written lists of core values, but we've seen numerous personal breakthroughs as a result of the process.

Understand that explaining the *whole* process would require its own book. However, here's a short introduction into that process. First, you have to begin by asking yourself six key questions:

1. In what nonwork environments are you highly engaged?
2. In what professional roles or jobs have you done your best work?
3. What help, advice, or qualities do others come to you for?
4. When have you been disengaged in a personal or professional setting?

5. What qualities in other people do you struggle with most?
6. What would you want said about you in your eulogy?

I recommend writing out your answers to each question on its own sheet of paper—six questions, six pages. Once you have a response to each question, identify certain keywords or phrases that appear in your responses to each question. For example:

- **Question:** What help, advice, or qualities do others come to you for?
- **Answer:** People ask me for candid advice on what they can do to improve. They expect me to share what they need to hear to get better, not what they want to hear to make them feel better.
- **Keywords:** Better, improve, candor, coaching.

One of the tests of a core value is that the opposite of the value tends to bother you on a visceral level. For questions that describe the opposite of your values, such as "What qualities in other people do you struggle with most?" you'll want to use keywords that describe the opposite of your responses. If you can't stand insincere people, you'd write *sincerity* or *authenticity* as a keyword. Once you've done this for each of the six questions, you'll have the beginning of a list of themes or keywords that begin to illuminate your core qualities. You'll likely notice that some of the same keywords come up in your responses to multiple questions. The more common a theme or keyword is across your responses, the more likely it is to be part of a core value.

For example, the sample response I just shared comes from my own work in this process. Keywords like *better, improve,* and *coaching* appear in my responses to several of the six questions shared earlier. My core value of "Find A Better Way and Share It" comes from these keywords and concepts.

Going through the process above, both for yourself and with your team, will begin to put you on a path that yields better personal and professional outcomes.

Since writing *Elevate,* this is by far the topic I am asked about most. If you are committed to doing this work, I have turned the full process we have used with our teams (and have continued to improve the process over the years) into a self-guided online course. It has already helped over fifteen hundred people discover their core values, and many leaders have also done this exercise with their teams. You can find that at **corevaluescourse.com**.

As a leader, finding your own core values is a great way to elevate your team's performance. It allows you to lead as your authentic self, clarify what matters most to your team, and get better results. However, you can compound these great outcomes when you coach your team on how to find their own core values.

Core Value Misalignment

A question I've been asked multiple times while sharing my core values exercise is *What if someone finds their core values aren't aligned with the organization and decides to leave as a result?*

This is rare, but it does happen. Discovering core values is the type of breakthrough that often causes a person to take stock of everything in their life—their lifestyle, their relationships, and yes, even their vocation or employer. The key is to determine whether any misalignment between personal core values and the organization or with a manager is workable or irreconcilable.

A person's core values don't need to be perfectly aligned with their organization. Instead, they need to decide whether they can still orient their life around those values while continuing to work at the company.

For example, a person may have a core value of "Express Myself Creatively." If this person is in a more operational role, they probably don't have a ton of opportunities for creative expression. The true passion that drives them may be something in art, music, or creative writing. However, even if this person cannot fulfill this need explicitly through their daily work, they may be happy working for an organization that gives them the flexibility they need to dedicate significant nonwork time to their artistic passion.

But in some cases, the value misalignment will be less navigable. I know this from experience.

In each of the jobs I had held since graduating from college, I always felt like something was missing or misaligned for me. I realized I did not like repeating the same tasks over and over, I wanted to have more control over my destiny, and I preferred taking calculated risks in pursuit of doing something that had not been done before. A job that allowed me to do those things was incredibly hard to find, and as a result, I was in dissatisfying roles where I was not doing my best work.

Now, it's very clear to me why I never found the right role. My core values—Self-Reliance, Find A Better Way and Share It, and Long-Term Orientation, specifically—were pointing to a clear conclusion: I needed to step into entrepreneurship to find professional fulfillment.

Naturally, I've recognized this same entrepreneurial passion in several of our employees at AP and have always encouraged people to take that leap if that is what they really want to do. People shouldn't deprive themselves of the path their core values are pointing them toward.

In other cases, there can be a more direct conflict between a company's core values and an employee's values. For example, one of our core values at AP is "Own It"—we expect employees to step up and take ownership of projects and outcomes and be willing to make important decisions on their own, sometimes with incomplete information. This aligns with being a client service organization in the fast-moving industry of digital marketing. For many people, this core value is energizing, especially for people who are self-directed, value autonomy, and don't require constant supervision or guidance.

But if an employee has a core value related to building consensus or including all perspectives, they might really struggle or clash with our "Own It" value. This will likely cause frustration in both directions—the employee is likely frustrated making decision without having the opportunity to run everything by their team and gain a consensus viewpoint and managers are frustrated that the employee struggles to take initiative and make independent decisions. These core misalignments are usually unfixable, as the parties value different things and it's best for both sides if the employee eventually moves on to an organization that better aligns with their values.

In other cases, the core value conflict occurs between employees and managers. While a manager and employee to do not need to align on all their values, they will probably struggle if they have direct conflicts on more than one value. It's important to understand that neither side is wrong in these conflicts—it's simply a case where a manager's core value happens to be the opposite of an employee's value. As with company-employee misalignment, it's best to avoid keeping misaligned managers and employees together long term and a move to another team might make all the difference.

It's true that, occasionally, an employee may leave the company after discovering their values, but this is the best outcome for everyone in the long run. If an employee's values are misaligned or unserved by their role or workplace, they will inevitably grow more unfulfilled the longer they stay. Issues or values misalignment never get better; they only grow more problematic over time. On the flip side, the employees who find their values are deeply aligned with the organization will often double down on their commitment and will likely feel more compelled to stay for the long haul.

Understanding Capabilities and Playing to Strengths

Admittedly, discovering your core values is deep, intense work, and it takes significant time investment to do it with a team. There are also some quicker and easier steps for building spiritual capacity and self-awareness.

Self-awareness doesn't just come from understanding principles such as core values—it also involves understanding strengths, weaknesses, and affinities. While we can often draw connections between our core values and strengths, in many cases a member of your team may have capabilities or tendencies that surprise you. To that extent, there are a number of self-serve assessments that help leaders and employees understand what they do well and where they can make the biggest impact.

There is a reason why so many personality, skill, and work-style assessments have popped up in the past several decades: teams are much more effective when people know what they are inherently good at, what their weaknesses are, and how they can use that awareness to best complement each other and improve communication. These assessments can also reveal breadcrumbs of information that may eventually lead to an understanding of values.

Over the years, we've used several assessments and tools to help our employees better understand their strengths, communication styles, and more. Some of my favorites include the DiSC assessment, the Kolbe A Index, and the CliftonStrengths assessment.

Other commonly used assessments include the Myers-Briggs Type Indicator and the Enneagram. While many people and organizations really like these programs, I personally have found them to be too complex for use across an organization without a deep level of commitment and repeated training with experts.

There's been some unease about the spread of personality testing in the workplace and the science behind some of these assessments. Some people also worry that they will be excluded from certain opportunities, or even certain jobs, based on their personality. I don't see these assessments as a scientific truth, and they should not be used to divide people into boxes or to seek out a preferred personality type. They're really designed to help people learn about tendencies, learning styles, and the types of interactions and work that are most fulfilling.

Assessments such as DiSC, Kolbe, and CliftonStrengths take little time to do and give your team some clarity on what they do well. Once team members have data from a few of these assessments, the results begin to illuminate patterns and helpful rubrics for explaining themselves to colleagues and understanding conflicts between employees or teams.

When two employees are experiencing friction in their work, they can often find the root of the tension in how their different lenses or tendencies lead to very different approaches. They can then use that knowledge to better understand each other and seek common ground.

One very important note— while many companies have specific assessments they use for hiring purposes, I would strongly caution against using these sort of assessments for this purpose for the following reasons:

▶ People tend to have an affinity for others who match their assessment results, even if it is an unconscious bias. A team or organization where everyone is similar will not be very well-rounded, nor will it see diverse perspectives and ideas brought to the surface.

▶ These assessments can't tell you everything about a person or predict how they'll behave in situations. I've seen introverts who are quiet and reserved by nature but thrive when they go on sales calls or present to clients. If you lean on archetype systems in evaluating candidates and employees, you are at risk of missing the fuller picture of who that person actually is and what they can bring to your team.

Instead of using these assessments as firm hiring and evaluation guidelines, leaders should use them to help their team communicate their expectations better, identify potential points of conflict, and mitigate possible points of friction before they become problematic.

As mentioned, one of the assessments we've had great results with is CliftonStrengths. Developed by former Gallup chairman Donald Clifton, CliftonStrengths evaluates employees on thirty-four key attributes and provides a ranking of which of these attributes they possess most prominently. These thirty-four strengths fall within four key buckets:[i]

► **Strategic Thinking:** Seeing the big picture, analyzing information, and using that knowledge to make sound decisions.

► **Influencing:** Taking charge, speaking up, getting the best ideas to the surface, and coordinating a team response.

► **Executing:** Getting things done, taking accountability for outcomes, and seeing things through to the end.

► **Relationship Building:** Building partnerships with other people, holding teams together, and making a group become greater than the sum of its parts.

The CliftonStrengths assessment helps people pinpoint exactly which of these buckets they are most aligned with and what their specific strengths are within those buckets. The best leaders maximize their people's strengths and minimize their weaknesses, and having a codified list of each employee's greatest strengths makes it easier to do that.

You can even use these strengths to dictate how you staff projects. You may want to combine someone who is strong in the Strategic Thinking bucket with someone strong in Executing; this combination will ensure that strategic decisions are thoughtfully made and executed. If you are building a team that needs to interface with a client or manage a key account, you would surely want to have at least one person who is strong in the Relationship Building bucket, as they can be trusted to build a strong bond with the client and make them feel valued.

At AP, we've gone as far as to have our entire company take the CliftonStrengths assessment at one of our annual summits. We had each person take the assessment, gave out individualized reports to each employee, and had a professional facilitator walk our full team through the definitions and applications of the various strengths. Then we had our employees break into groups with their functional teams to compare their results and brainstorm how they could use them to work together more effectively. Giving our team this self-awareness and the vocabulary to articulate their natural strengths and weaknesses led to better collaboration beyond the summit.

Allowing your people to identify and lean into their strengths will put them on a path to doing their best work while simultaneously gaining awareness on how they can work more effectively with others.

Understanding Your Why

Of all the personal assessments I've encountered, the one that I have found most powerful and closely connected to core values is the Why Archetype assessment. We went through the assessment process with a facilitator as management team years ago, and it's the thing we refer to most often in our daily work to understand and solve conflicts, divide and conquer responsibilities, and communicate effectively.

The concept of a Why was popularized several years ago by leadership expert Simon Sinek. As Sinek shared in his bestselling book *Start with Why*, each person is motivated intrinsically by a core purpose that is the driving force across their personal and professional lives. Sinek described how our Why is rooted in our limbic system, the part of our brain responsible for feelings, instinctive decisions, and natural tendencies. The limbic system also produces what we like to call "gut feelings," instincts that we can't quite articulate or understand but that feel undeniable in the moment. A person's Why is logical and cannot be artificial; it is who they are instinctively and dictates how they reflexively respond in most situations.[ii]

Sinek's work was thought provoking, but he ultimately left the reader to face an enormous question without an easy framework to help find the answer. Finding your why, as it turns out, is not something most people can do by themselves.

This is where Gary Sanchez, an entrepreneur and CEO, stepped in to fill the void. He developed a collection of nine Why archetypes that serve as an effective way to understand our core motivations. Sanchez founded the WHY Institute and created a helpful assessment people can use to determine their own Why archetype. Having now worked with these archetypes for almost ten years, I have found them to be incredibly accurate and predictive of an individual's primary mode of operation. They are as follows:[iii]

- To Contribute to a Greater Cause
- To Build Trust
- To Make Sense of Complex Situations
- To Find a Better Way
- To Do Things the Right Way
- To Challenge the Status Quo
- To Build Mastery
- To Create Clarity
- To Simplify

My Why archetype, "To Find a Better Way," not surprisingly, closely aligns to my dominant core value, "Find a Better Way and Share It." It's a primary motivator for me and related to what I do best. It also identifies places where I have conflict in my personal and professional life as a why can turn from a strength to a weakness when over indexed.

I speak regularly to companies and conferences, including virtually. Typically, I use standard presentations for my various speech topics but adjust them for each client to suit their theme or keynote preferences.

Once, I joined a virtual keynote presentation, showing up

ten minutes early for a last-minute tech check. As I skimmed through my slides to ensure they displayed properly on the videoconferencing platform, I suddenly had a few ideas for last-minute improvements I really wanted to make. You can imagine the anxious look on the organizer's face as my Chief of Staff and I made several edits to the deck I would be presenting just a few minutes later. In moments like this, I am inherently focused on how to make something just a bit better to deliver the best possible outcome, rather than the tight timeline.

Similarly, I am a constant tinkerer, often suggesting edits and improvements to products, strategic plans, and presentations up until the last minute. I have a very hard time leaving well enough alone. When our company hits a milestone, I'm usually inclined to look toward what we can improve going forward or eying the next challenge. As a result, I am not good at celebrating wins, and that is an issue as a leader, especially for people on my team who deserve that recognition of a job well done.

Over the years, I had to learn that if I try to make everything better all the time in our organization, I will just exhaust and wear people out. Plus, we may lose sight of accomplishing the few things that count most, which is counterproductive to my core motivation. I need to check myself to ensure my urge to make every little thing better doesn't prevent us from making the most important things better.

This tendency also shows up outside work. Once I discovered my own Why, I naturally wanted my family to identify theirs as well so they could get better. My wife's Why is "To Do Things the Right Way." As you can imagine, this can really conflict with my own Why, especially when Rachel is convinced she has identified the right way to do something, but I continue to fixate on trying to make it better.

Knowing the difference between our Whys gives us a clear, mutually understood vocabulary to navigate the conflicts our natural tendencies cause. Occasionally, when she has a well-planned vacation itinerary, a dinner reservation, or a weekend activity, she'll explicitly say to me, "Please, don't try to make it better."

Hearing her say that reminds me to keep my better way instincts in check. It isn't always easy, but at least I know what she needs from me in that moment.

On the other hand, Rachel occasionally agonizes over decisions, even in mundane situations, such as what she should order for dinner, which is a very common struggle for a Right Way Why. In these cases, I might reference *her* Why by saying lightheartedly, "There's no *right* answer. You just have to choose."

Without this vocabulary, it would be easy for us to get frustrated with each other's tendencies or default approach. Having this language and framework when one of us is leaning too far into our Why improves our communication and helps mitigate logical and predictable conflicts that result from our different frames of reference.

The same thing is true in my business. Knowing that my Why is "To Find a Better Way" also allows me to explain to my team how I approach different situations. For example, I am often likely to be thinking about improvements or future goals—it's just my nature to be thinking ahead. This does not mean I am unhappy with what is being done currently.

Along those same lines, knowing my Why allows members of my team to effectively manage up and respond to me. A team member who knows my urge to find and suggest improvements will recognize that I occasionally suggest ideas that are impractical to implement or may distract from more important priorities. That employee might say to me, "I am happy to do this. However, making that improvement would mean pausing work on one of our other projects. What would you like me to pause?"

This illustrates how my team has used knowledge of my Why to ensure that my instinct to make things better doesn't compromise our most important work.

Because a person's Why is core to their motivation and behavioral tendencies, it tends to show up everywhere. Knowing and using that language in everyday communication helps create better clarity within a team.

Using the Why Archetype assessment to build this type of shared understanding between leaders and their teams is something we do with as many of our managers as possible, and it's a key part of our leadership training. We even dedicate at least half a day to helping new managers discover their Whys at our leadership workshops.

In the past, scaling the Why concept to more people across the organization was challenging—a person needed to sit for a brief conversation with an experienced facilitator to determine their Why. However, today there is actually a self-serve assessment that Sanchez and his team have developed at the WHY Institute, which is available at **robertglazer.com/eyt-resources**.

We're already discussing how to make this Why Archetype assessment a bigger part of our training for our whole team.

A Self-Aware Organization

At the beginning of this chapter, I shared the story of Andrew, a manager who had a significant breakthrough during a core value exercise. Andrew's realization that self-awareness was a nonnegotiable core value was eye-opening, but the real effects of that revelation came after the workshop. Andrew realized he had to align his daily leadership to his self-awareness core value by communicating his most important principles to his team, which in itself was a function of self-awareness.

Andrew gave a detailed presentation to his team in the weeks following the workshop. He shared his core values and what each one meant in a leadership context. He made commitments to his team for what he would do and what direct reports could expect from him as a leader. Finally, and perhaps more importantly, he shared what he needed members of their team to do to make their manager-employee relationship a success. Each need was clearly tied to a value—the manager learned how to use his core values to explain what was most important to him and how it impacted his team. This presentation was so effective that we share it with workshop attendees as a template worth emulating.

Andrew is one of nearly one hundred people who have gone through our advanced leadership training workshop. They've done the core values exercise shared earlier, identified their Whys, and even taken the CliftonStrengths assessment to determine their top five strengths. Even though we don't teach tactical management techniques in this specific workshop, leaders who attend almost always see an increase in their management feedback scores from employees.

Ultimately, building your team's spiritual capacity is about clarity and alignment. Your goal should be to help your people understand what is most important to them and how they work best, then help them use those findings to guide their daily work.

Plus, helping your leaders have this level of clarity allows their teams to adapt their actions so they can work more seam-lessly with their leader. It is much easier for a team to deliver the best results to their manager if they know what the manager values most and vice versa.

Helping an employee discover and understand this informa-tion helps them develop into an authentic, confident, capable leader rather than a cookie-cutter manager following a company script. And gaining the type of self-awareness that comes from high spiritual capacity isn't just beneficial for leaders and man-agers. It's also a great tool to help individual contributors deter-mine how they can contribute at the highest level. Organizations work better when employees work on projects and in roles that leverage their strengths and tendencies.

As a leader, you have the ability to help your people discover their best path, creating significant benefits for both your team and the organization along the way. Building spiritual capacity is the foundation.

ACTION STEPS

Finding Core Values
► Help your direct reports start thinking about their core values. If you have identified your own values,

consider sharing how they've shaped your personal and professional life and the results you've gotten.

▸ Take the hour-long Core Values Course to help discover your personal core values and unlock your own spiritual capacity or as an exercise with your team. **You can use the code "eytbook" at checkout to get a $10 discount—learn more at corevaluescourse.com.**

Other Valuable Assessments

▸ Consider doing any of these assessments with your team, department, or even entire organization to help uncover strengths, weakness, and communication styles. Links to all three of the assessments below are available at **robertglazer.com/eyt-resources**:

» **Why Institute's Why Assessment**
» **Clifton Strengths Finder**
» **DiSC Behavior Assessment**

Chapter Three

BUILD YOUR TEAM'S INTELLECTUAL CAPACITY

*"I am always doing what I can't do yet in
order to learn how to do it."*

—Vincent van Gogh

A smirk came across my face as I read the email I'd been expecting for some time. Within a few seconds, I sent my reply without having to think twice: "Come work for me."

I knew I wasn't quite following our hiring process and I was going to get in trouble for it, but this was a rare case where it was better to ask for forgiveness rather than permission.

It was 2018, and the email was from a staff member of a professional organization whom I'd worked with many times over the past few years, planning several leadership training events. In that time, he and I had developed a strong personal and professional relationship.

He was the type of employee organizations love and don't want to lose. Though just a few years out of school, he was very smart and showed a voracious appetite for learning. Plus, he constantly offered to take on new projects above his level and out of his comfort zone.

During his several years at the organization, I saw him improve on a fast trajectory, earning the respect of members, colleagues, and company leaders alike. A few people joked that if he chose to stay long term, they would eventually be working for him.

I always knew he would be a great fit for our team, but did not want to solicit him from the organization. I also knew, in the back of my mind, that he was growing at a faster rate than the organization and would eventually hit an inflection point where he'd feel compelled to move on. I decided to let nature run its course.

He emailed me that day to share that he planned to leave the organization and wanted to get my advice on next steps for his career. His choice to leave was not an easy one; he had close friends on the organization's staff and a strong relationship with his manager, and he genuinely enjoyed his work. He couldn't explain the pull he felt to do something new, but he sensed that if he stayed at the organization, he would regret it years later.

He'd hit the exact inflection point I expected: he had stopped learning and growing, and he was afraid of stagnating.

When we spoke, I told him I would be happy to offer him advice but even happier to offer him a job. I added that if he came to work for me, he would never be bored for a single day.

Today, Mick is my Chief of Staff, editor of the book you are reading now, and coauthor of one of my recent books, *How to Thrive in the Virtual Workplace*.

While Mick may be a rare employee, his situation was hardly unique. Having an opportunity to learn and grow is a crucial driver of employee satisfaction and retention, and people tend to eye the exits when they stop learning.

In his research, *New York Times* bestselling author Daniel Pink discovered that mastery is one of the three core pillars of intrinsic motivation. Most people have an internal drive to improve at what they do—to learn, to grow, to get better. Therefore stagnation, even at a high level of achievement, can cause restlessness. People want to work at organizations that help them feed this desire to improve.

The numbers back this up. In 2019, a global LinkedIn survey found that 94 percent of employees claim they would stay at a job longer if given more chances to learn. The survey found this thirst for learning is especially present in millennial and Gen Z employees, who stated that having opportunities to learn is the number one thing that makes them happy at work.[i]

Star performers in particular are often the most voracious learners and typically crave new challenges and active coaching. This presents a paradox for many organizations: the most promising employees can also be the toughest to keep satiated. If the rate of the change of an employee exceeds that of the company or industry, the end is likely near for that employee's tenure.

Organizations must either find a way to consistently give their rising stars opportunities to learn and grow or risk losing them to a competitor who will. This is where the second element of capacity building comes into play: intellectual capacity.

Intellectual capacity is about how you improve your ability to think, learn, plan, and execute with discipline. In an organizational context, companies with high intellectual capacity are constantly helping their employees learn new skills, build better habits, achieve personal and professional goals, learn from feedback, and coach each other to improve.

In theory, this capacity should be the easiest for organizations to prioritize, because so many already have training and professional development programs. But that's only the theory. In practice, many organizations fall short of creating a culture of continuous learning. Organizational cultures that are learning-driven are often prone to disruption—as leaders and employees learn and grow, they often push new ideas, initiatives, and strategies in a constant effort to make the organization better. Many organizations don't want the boat constantly rocked in this way and feel more comfortable focusing on the here and now.

Learning and disruption go hand in hand—they cannot be stratified. However, this link is often beneficial, even if it causes momentary discomfort. To illustrate, I'll draw from a concept called the S-curve, a mainstay business principle of product adoption that has been recently popularized for personal development by *Wall Street Journal* bestselling author and executive coach Whitney Johnson.

Essentially, the S-curve is a way of plotting our development in any given skill or role. When we are learning a new skill or adjusting to a new professional role, our progress is slow at first—we are at the bottom of the S-curve in the inexperience stage. Then we reach the middle of the S-curve—the engagement phase, where our progress accelerates. Once we have laid a learning foundation, we begin to grow exponentially toward the final phase: mastery. It's often during this period of acceleration that we experience the fastest growth and are most engaged, as we push toward the top of the curve. We know enough about what we are doing to have confidence but not so much that it has become mundane or automatic.

S CURVE OF LEARNING

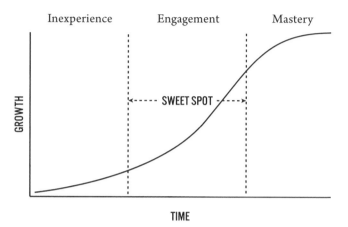

Inexperience   Engagement   Mastery

GROWTH

SWEET SPOT

TIME

Johnson, Whitney. "Manage Your Organization as a Portfolio of Learning Curves." *Harvard Business Review*, January/February 2022. https://hbr.org/2022/01/manage-your-organization-as-a-portfolio-of-learning-curves.

Many companies' shortcomings in talent development can be demonstrated with the S-curve. These organizations understandably think their responsibility is to guide each employee to the top of their current S-curves. Johnson has found the top of the S-curve is a dangerous area, because it's where employees are most likely to plateau and become bored or complacent.

The way to avoid this stagnation is to jump to a new S-curve—trading the comfort of mastery for the exciting upward slope of a new curve and a new challenge.

Sure, some people are satisfied with mastering a single S-curve and resting at the top. But after almost twenty years of hiring and developing talent, I've consistently found the highest performers are never satisfied with mastery of just one hill—they will instinctively want to embrace the challenge of climbing a new one.

To be fair, not everyone in an organization wants to be constantly climbing a new learning curve, and organizations do need a steady number of employees who are content doing what they do at a high level. At the same time, a growing company or team in a competitive marketplace will need to set a culture of learning and development.

Unless you're a monopolistic business with no competition—and congratulations if you are—most companies cannot maintain their status quo for long before a competitor is fast on their heels. The business world and business cycles move so quickly today that for most companies, if you're not willing to disrupt yourself, you are on a path toward irrelevance. Building intellectual capacity creates the right type of disruption, on an individual and organizational level.

Before we dig into how to build intellectual capacity in your organization, I'll share a helpful metaphor. Think of intellectual capacity as a person's individual operating system. It's the software that guides your hardware and determines how well it performs: how you process and respond to new information, how you organize and prioritize, and whether you have the right knowledge and habits to reach your goals.

When you upgrade your personal operating system, you can get more done, not because you are doing more but because you process the same inputs with more efficiency and less energy. You're optimizing your performance.

Our operating systems are universal across our personal and professional lives. For example, I don't know many people who are disorganized, unmotivated, and constantly tardy outside work but precise, driven, and time-disciplined in the workplace.

This means that building intellectual capacity, as with all the capacities, is holistic. When people apply good learning processes, habits, routines, and standards on one side of the work-life scale, they see similar improvement in those same areas in the other. Helping your employees build intellectual capacity outside work brings demonstrable value to your workplace.

Creating a Culture of Learning

One of the reasons I was never a great student in elementary school or high school is that I was frequently bored and unengaged. As with many future entrepreneurs, I hated sitting still and paying attention for long periods of time. I enjoyed challenging established principles and being creative rather than memorizing facts and data. It wasn't until I discovered my passion for business and marketing that I realized I loved to learn all along. I simply hadn't been in the right learning environment—both in terms of subject matter and learning style.

Most people's drive to learn is informed by their environment. If you want people in your organization to be constantly growing, create a culture that encourages and supports learning and development in different ways. And you shouldn't just focus on how to make your employees better at their jobs today. Instead, you should think ahead for the roles they may ascend to and tap into what motivates and interests them.

As a leader, building an environment where everyone is encouraged to learn and is both implicitly and explicitly rewarded for it is one of the best investments of your organization's and leaders' time, energy, and resources. This chapter is a detailed guide on how to do this.

TRAINING BEYOND THE JOB DESCRIPTION

Most organizations have some form of on-the-job training that, not surprisingly, teaches employees how to do their job. However, for too many organizations, that is where training begins and ends. Organizations and teams with high intellectual capacity don't just focus on an employee's current role— they think ahead to the employee's future and consider how to broaden their base of learning and knowledge.

Take finance as an example. Each new employee today who starts at AP joins a basic finance training with our CFO. As an open-book organization, our employees see the same financials as the executive team, and we want to make sure they understand them.

In these finance trainings, not only do employees learn about the key financial targets we monitor, but they also learn about general accounting concepts such as a balance sheet, a cash-flow statement, and an income statement.

I should be clear: becoming an "open-book organization" is a place where I did a total 180 from my position when the company started. I used to be terrified by the idea of letting people peek behind our financial curtain. I thought giving people the full picture would prompt unwanted questions and cause more problems than it was worth, so we went out of our way to avoid sharing our financial data.

This is an example of an area where I was dead wrong, and I learned from others that there was a better way. Accountability was a key part of our core values, but how could we expect people to be accountable for things they did not know or understand?

Shifting to open-book management didn't lead to problems and uncomfortable conversations. Instead it built trust and helped us create metrics and incentives around the desired outcomes.

These financial trainings, while high level, create a tangible increase in our team's financial literacy. Most employees don't need to understand the company's macro finances to do their specific jobs. However, getting a deeper understanding of our company financial engine gives employees better context for making financial decisions and understanding the implications their individual and team outputs have on the company's bottom line.

For example, when an employee is managing a project and is responsible for the budget, their understanding of the company's finances may inform their decision-making, especially when their bonus is tied to the company's performance. They might suggest reducing the budget or increasing it in different cases if they understand the dependent variables. It's really hard to ask people to make decisions in the best interest of the business when they don't understand the full financial picture, so we do our best to give them both the information and knowledge to understand that data.

In broadening their employees' base of learning, companies should also strongly consider investing time and resources in training the future organizational leaders to lead, even before their first promotion to manager.

This should be obvious, but I've seen plenty of organizations offer management and leadership training only after their employees begin in management roles, and in some cases only after they've received negative feedback on their management style. This is a bit like teaching a person to drive a race car in the middle of the Daytona 500.

Here's a fact that should not be a surprise: most first-time managers aren't very good at managing when they start, and few things drive employee turnover more than ineffective management. Putting newer managers in a position to succeed through preemptive training helps prevent talent losses on those managers' teams.

At AP, we offer general management training to employees at all levels of the organization, even if they don't manage a person or team yet. Today, we host three-part virtual management training sessions where members of our executive team share the most effective leadership and management tactics they have discovered from their personal experiences, and they also share mistakes and lessons from their leadership journey. Topics include the following:

▸ How to manage in a remote environment and hold teams accountable when you don't share a workspace with them
▸ Strategies for delegating, avoiding micromanagement, increasing vulnerability, and empowering team members to take on more responsibility
▸ Strategies for clear, effective communication to ensure directions are clear and understood
▸ Leading with authenticity and intention rather than simply copying another manager's approach

▸ How to identify and address underperformance preemptively, before it becomes unfixable, and deliver feedback in a respectful way

These presentations are designed to give employees an understanding of the skills they will need so they are able to practice them both before and after they step into a management role. For example, we don't want our managers to learn how to delegate only after they've been labeled a micromanager by their direct reports in their first review.

We also host Manager Forums, where employees are sorted into small groups that meet monthly for six months. Just as in our management training presentations, members of our executive team facilitate these Manager Forums. In each meeting, the facilitator shares a tactical management lesson that employees can use in their own work. The rest of the time is reserved for confidential discussions, where forum members can share a professional challenge they're working through, and everyone in the group helps them solve the problem.

Though these are called Manager Forums, every AP employee is given the option to join one, whether they manage someone or not. While the tactical management lessons won't be pertinent to all employees in the moment, we still want to share these lessons with our individual contributors and rising stars.

This has a dual effect. First, it gives these nonmanagers a foundation of managerial knowledge to draw from if and when they do become managers someday. Second, it piques their curiosity about management and leadership and may encourage them to seek and engage with more resources to learn about these topics.

We've had several nonmanagers proactively seek out further learning opportunities after being exposed to these topics in these forums, and these people are usually the ones who end up becoming managers—and good ones.

In addition to the live trainings, we have also built up several resource centers for ongoing leadership and management training organized around important management and leadership concepts. We have robust lists of top management and leadership books and articles, curated podcasts on important topics, and professional development opportunities, courses, and conferences that we point people to for independent study.

And then there is our aforementioned flagship program, the advanced leadership training workshops. At these retreats, ten to twenty up-and-coming leaders gather together for two to three days of intense leadership training. Generally, these sessions are not overly tactical. As described in the previous chapter, we start with building spiritual capacity as the foundation.

I believe there is no better use of our time and resources than helping the future leaders of the organization better learn how to lead. And it's best to begin before they grab the leadership torch rather than struggling to learn on the job.

FOSTERING PERSONAL LEARNING

While company-directed learning is one aspect of building a learning-focused culture, learning should not just be top-down. Encourage your team to come together and pick topics that they are passionate about as a group or as individuals.

One common approach is encouraging or sponsoring a company book club. You can either buy books for a group of employees who meet to discuss the book of their choosing and/or create a list of books or audiobooks that cover valuable topics and allow your employees to get reimbursed for buying those books.

These books don't always have to be related directly to work. Studies have found reading improves memory and concentration and relieves stress, regardless of what you're actually reading.[ii] If you're looking for books that will help you and your team build capacity, I have a list that I update periodically, which is linked at **robertglazer.com/eyt-resources**.

Podcasts are also an increasingly popular way to both learn and share knowledge from some of the world's best minds. Plus, best of all, most of them are free. Personally, I've learned more from long-form episodes of *The Tim Ferriss Show*, a podcast with close to a billion downloads to date, then I've learned in entire years of schooling.

View podcasts the same way you view books—educational resources that are worth sharing. You might create a list of informative podcast episodes that share best practices on important topics and encourage employees to add to the resource list. You can also start a podcast club, where team members listen to the same episode once per month and meet to discuss it, similar to a book club.

I have also used podcast episodes as key framing devices to help prepare for strategic conversations. Recently, to lay the groundwork for a brainstorming session on Web3 and the metaverse, I encouraged the team to listen to an episode of Ferriss's show on the topic with several leading experts. It was a great way for them to get their hands around a dense topic in less time than it would've taken them to read a series of white papers or books.

Another very popular learning driver is direct educational reimbursements, which have become increasingly popular and are offered by leading companies such as Amazon, Walmart,

Apple, Deloitte, and Disney. Many organizations give each employee a set budget per year that they can use to subsidize professional certifications, tuition for pursuit of a degree, or even registration fees for online courses or in-person trainings. Removing these educational barriers demonstrates your commitment to your employees' learning and growth.

While you might be tempted to restrict education reimbursements to ensure they are work related, there is a strong argument for doing the opposite and encouraging employees to learn more about anything that is of interest to them.

There's research that supports this as well. Author David Epstein has found that building knowledge and expertise in one area leads to growth in other disciplines as well. Helping an employee invest in learning something they are passionate about can actually unlock better performance at work because insights gleaned in one area can often be applied to another. Epstein clarifies the value of this knowledge transfer in his book, *Range*: "Learners become better at applying their knowledge to a situation they've never seen before, which is the essence of creativity."[iii]

Building these types of training programs and learning initiatives takes both time and financial investment. However, the result is an organizational culture where employees feel like learning is not just encouraged but imperative to success, which raises the bar for everyone. Plus, they will associate working at your organization with expanding their capacity and career opportunities, which is a virtuous cycle.

Holistic Discipline

Remember the earlier notion that an operating system is the same in both personal and professional life? To illustrate this, picture two people: Emily and Frank. Both are managers who work from home.

- ▸ Emily's day begins with an alarm at 7:00 a.m. She meditates for fifteen minutes, then showers and has a leisurely breakfast, reading the newspaper as she finishes her coffee. By 8:00 a.m., she's at her computer feeling fresh, focused, and ready to start the day.
- ▸ Frank's alarm goes off at 7:50 a.m., but he snoozes it until 8:05. He groggily scrolls through work emails in bed and remembers he has an 8:30 a.m. call with his direct report that he forgot about. He frantically showers and sits down for work just in time to join the call. Frank's direct report feels like they don't have Frank's full attention.
- ▸ Emily has taken a few minutes to write down the most important things she has to accomplish during the workday and then designate time blocks during the day for each

of those priorities. She joins a one-on-one check-in with a direct report and has a productive conversation with clear next steps. Because Emily has blocked off time for her most important priorities, she gets everything crucial done by noon and decides to walk to a café for lunch with a friend before continuing her workday.

▸ Frank spends most of his morning reading emails and watching his inbox, responding right away to a bunch of low-priority messages. At 10:30 a.m., he feels himself totally losing focus and realizes it's because he hasn't eaten or had coffee—his morning was so frantic that he skipped breakfast entirely. By noon, Frank hasn't accomplished anything substantial, and he has a full slate of calls on his calendar for the afternoon. The day already feels lost.

This is an extreme illustration of a crucial point—personal routines and habits have an enormous impact on professional performance. The courses of Emily's and Frank's hypothetical workdays are determined before business hours have even begun: Emily's structured, positive morning routine has her showing up to work clearheaded and ready to attack the day, and Frank's frantic morning rush leaves him frayed, unprepared, and reactive.

People who are disorganized and undisciplined outside the workday will usually show up similarly in the workplace,

ELEVATE YOUR TEAM

especially in a world where work is increasingly performed from home. This is why organizations have a huge opportunity to make competences such as time management, organization, prioritization, and discipline part of their training and development programs. The more employees develop and practice these core skills, the better their performance and the better the results.

BUILDING ROUTINES AND HABITS

I can't think of a skill more important to company productivity than time management and organization. When new employees join AP, one of the first things we do is teach best practices for managing their inbox. For example, we offer the following tips:

▶ Be thoughtful about which notifications you leave on and when they are active, especially if you are prone to distraction. Most people don't need a visual or audible notification for every e-mail, Slack message, or text they receive.

▶ Evaluate which emails require an immediate response and which ones can be reserved for later. We recommend that when an employee sees an email on a highly urgent topic— such as where the sender clarifies that they need a response immediately—they should respond in the moment rather than leaving it for later and running the risk of missing a deadline.

68

▸ **Set a two-minute rule for inbound emails.** If an employee can respond to an email in under two minutes, we recommend they do so immediately. If it requires more time, it's worth setting aside for later, when the employee can dedicate more time to respond.

▸ Use folders for specific projects or topics and set up email rules that automatically file messages into those folders. Then, employees can respond to emails in those folders in batches.

▸ Set aside blocks of time to clear out the inbox a few times a day rather than being constantly interrupted during focused work. This is when it's best to respond to those emails that take more than two minutes to answer.

Keeping an inbox under control doesn't just keep colleagues and clients happy. It is also a disciplined keystone habit that guides employees to practice building structure into their workday. It's like the professional version of making your bed each morning.

A second key technique was highlighted in Emily's story at the beginning of this section: time blocking. This is a method of scheduling where you set aside specific times of the day for certain tasks tied to your most important priorities. You may, for example, have blocks for emails, focused work on key priorities, meetings, and even lunch, breaks, and exercise. Time blocking works because it gives employees more control over their schedules and makes it more likely that the most important tasks are accomplished. It also discourages frequent interruptions and unnecessary meetings.

To encourage time blocking throughout your organization, leaders should model it for their teams by sharing their calendars and showing how they schedule and protect their time. A tactic I've found successful is setting GSD, or Get Stuff Done, time. This is time that employees can put in their calendars to signal to colleagues that they are not to be disturbed so they can put their heads down for focused work on key deliverables. I dedicate a portion of each day to GSD time and encourage my team to do so as well.

On a given day, my schedule might look like this:

▸ 9:00 a.m. to 12:00 p.m.: GSD Time (I try to schedule this in the morning, when I am cognitively my sharpest.)
▸ 12:00 p.m. to 1:00 p.m.: Break (lunch and exercise)
▸ 1:00 p.m. to 3:00 p.m.: One-On-One Meetings/Check-Ins
▸ 3:00 p.m. to 3:30 p.m.: Afternoon Break (I try my best not to give this break time away, as it's important.)
▸ 3:30 p.m. to 5:30 p.m.: Group Calls/Meetings
▸ 5:30 p.m. to 6:30 p.m.: Kids' Sports

Time management and organization are holistic skills. Once your people start using better time management techniques, they'll find they are able to get more done in less time. The more they experience this efficiency advantage, the more they'll be dedicated to practicing these skills, both inside and outside work.

MORNINGS MATTER

Another highly important practice is a good morning routine. As we saw with our story of Emily and Frank, the way your employees start their day can often make or break the workday before they even sit down at a desk.

It's been widely reported that so many of the world's top performers—in all walks of life—have a morning routine with some mix of exercise, reading, journaling, and meditation. You'll notice scrolling through social media, watching cable news, or reading work email in bed are not on the menu.

In *Elevate*, I shared that I developed a morning routine largely based on the SAVERS routine highlighted in Hal Elrod's hit book *The Miracle Morning*. Elrod recommends dedicating thirty to sixty minutes to these six actions:[iv]

- ▶ Silence (meditation)
- ▶ Affirmations
- ▶ Visualization
- ▶ Exercising

▶ Reading

▶ Scribing (journaling)

Convincing your employees to adopt a strong morning routine might seem beyond the scope of an employer's purview; however, it fits very logically in the scope of leadership training. For example, when we hold leadership training workshops for our team members, we ask each attendee to try a simple morning routine each day of the program. They spend ten minutes meditating, ten minutes reading, and ten minutes journaling first thing each morning, then we gather for thirty minutes of exercise as a group. A training program is a natural place to test this out—the attendees are already in the headspace of wanting to improve and learn. And if the workshop is held off-site, they'll be able to try the routine in a neutral environment, without partners, children, or pets possibly distracting them.

The feedback has always been positive, but it comes with a common objection: many parents of young kids who are short on sleep already struggle to imagine getting up any earlier than they must. For them, I offer a simple challenge: try getting up just fifteen minutes earlier to gain fifteen minutes of quiet "me time." Waking up with screaming kids as an alarm clock or to some situation that requires parenting attention does not help people start the day with a positive, productive mindset.

Pretty much every time, employees who try this experiment find the results rewarding. Many find that they enjoy their calm mornings so much that they get up earlier than they'd have ever expected to give themselves more personal time.

How your team spends their mornings doesn't seem like a professional concern, but how we spend the first minutes of the day resonates throughout the day. This is the essence of intellectual capacity: incremental improvements that yield significant results, personally and professionally.

MASTERING GOAL SETTING

The final piece of a disciplined, organized career and life is goal setting. Think of a person you admire, who always seems to accomplish everything they want and who makes it look easy. Chance are they are very intentional about setting goals and building processes that build toward those goals. The same is true for companies.

Setting and achieving goals isn't an innate skill—it's more like a muscle that is built through experience and effort. And, not surprisingly, an effective goal-setting process looks almost identical when used by both individuals and organizations.

Every organizational management system I've tested or examined, such as Entrepreneurial Operating System (EOS), Gazelles, or OKR, is built on the same principle of setting strategic long-term goals or objectives, then reverse engineering the shorter-term milestones and actions that build toward those larger objectives.

Because of this, it's very helpful for your employees to be able to connect the dots between a goal and the actions that build toward it. For example, a three-year objective should be broken down into one-year goals and then quarterly goals that all build to the multiyear objective when completed.

Spend time talking to your employees about their goals and coaching them on how they can get there by thinking big, sharing their goals, creating accountability, and staying the course with discipline. My experience is that doing this creates both personal wins and more excitement about pursuing company goals. If an employee achieves a big personal goal through a clearly defined plan, the BHAGs—big, hairy, audacious goals— that you set for your company will feel more attainable through that same process.

Here's a great example: at one of our annual events, we asked a group of employees to set and share their personal goals with as much specificity and action orientation as possible. We asked them to picture themselves in the future and imagine what they would want to have accomplished. We taught them the concept of SMART goals—objectives that are specific, measurable, achievable, relevant, and time-bound—to help them focus their brainstorming.

After the event, we also created a channel in our company Slack where employees were encouraged to share their personal goals for the upcoming year. This was beneficial for two reasons. First, writing down a goal is a great way to articulate the objective and turn it into something tangible and attainable. Second, putting the goal in Slack created public accountability—by sharing their goal with colleagues in a permanent place, an employee felt more motivated to accomplish that objective. As we did this exercise, many members of our team shared that they had never created or shared goals publicly before, but they demonstrated vulnerability around personal goals related to health, fitness, relationships, wealth, and more.

One employee in particular set a goal to get back into photography, including buying a camera and taking a photography class, which she had wanted to do for some time. This led to one of the best examples of the utility of sharing goals and the power of the law of attraction. The employee printed out her photography goal and put it on her wall above her desk. Though she did this to keep the goal in her focus, someone else noticed: her partner, who bought both the camera and the photography class for her as a Mother's Day gift.

Organizational habits, daily routines, and even personal goal setting may not seem like obvious priorities for your organization, but they all lead toward the same end—bringing

ELEVATE YOUR TEAM

productive, consistent structure to our daily lives, which allows us to accomplish more with less time and energy.

Coaching and Feedback

Jane shifted back uncomfortably in her chair as the words from her boss, Mark, sank in.

"This isn't easy to say, but I just want to be really clear with you that if we don't see a sustained improvement in your performance around the key issues we discussed today, it's very likely we are going to be speaking about a transition out of the company."

Jane finally understood the gravity of the situation, and Mark was able to confidently communicate a message that no leader looks forward to giving.

That's when I interrupted and said "freeze" and asked the other twenty people in the room for feedback.

This was the last day of one of our advanced leadership training workshops, and we were doing a "difficult conversations" role-playing exercise. We crafted a selection of prompts that were based on real performance management conversation topics, and we assigned volunteers to act out each role—with one person playing the manager (Mark) and the other playing the direct report (Jane). The conversation topics were ripped-from-the-headlines types of situations—complicated performance management conversations that all our managers eventually have to navigate and that many workshop attendees would likely need to have for the first time in their careers in the next year as new managers. Even though these were low-stakes role-playing exercises, the fictional managers felt real discomfort and often struggled to communicate clearly and stay on script in the moment.

We've done this exercise multiple times, with over one hundred employees at this point. As part of the session, we always have a volunteer pretend to be a manager who needs to inform their direct report in a check-in that their job is at risk if they don't improve, and we have another volunteer play an employee who thinks things are going well.

Usually, the two have a cordial conversation where the manager references some things the direct report can do better and reminds them to improve their time management and communication precision. The result of that uncertainty is the employee assumes everything is going well overall, even though it isn't. That's an outcome we most want to avoid, and it's the impetus of the exercise. While the audience has read each volunteer's prompts, the role-players themselves know only their side of the story, to imitate a real-life situation.

About ten minutes into the conversation, I tell our role-players to freeze and ask the audience for their input. The first question I ask is, "Raise your hand if you think the manager has made it clear that the direct report's job is on the line." Every time, not a single hand is raised.

And now everyone clearly sees the communication disconnect that often leads to disaster: the manager thinks the employee has gotten the message, and the employee is on a path to being blindsided.

Giving this type of feedback and warning is extremely difficult. I know many seasoned leaders who absolutely agonize over these types of conversations, even after having been part of them many times.

While it's understandable—and very human—to find these conversations wrenching, they are even harder if you haven't learned how to have them. Plus, the pain that's avoided by dodging these conversations is nothing compared to the damage that results when two people think they are on the same page about a crucial issue when they in fact are not at all.

A new manager who spends hours contemplating how to deliver difficult news or loses sleep for a week before a conversation like this is wasting a lot of valuable time and energy that impacts their work in other areas. That's exactly why role-playing these types of conversations is so important—we want our people to practice these discussions in a low-stakes environment, and we want them to observe sample conversations to see what traps to avoid and what best practices to emulate. When the unfortunate but inevitable time comes to have one of these conversations, they will be much better prepared, less nervous, and hopefully able to achieve a better outcome for everyone involved. It could also mean avoiding spending ten to twenty hours of extra time planning for a performance conversation or spending even more time cleaning up the mess after a poorly executed discussion.

This is another example of improving the operating system: getting a better outcome with less energy.

BUILDING A CULTURE OF FEEDBACK

A culture with high intellectual capacity is also highly dependent on consistent, direct feedback. A learning culture is by definition a feedback culture; one cannot be decoupled from the other. If managers are not able to deliver feedback to help their teams improve—or if employees believe they can ignore feedback without consequence—there is a ceiling on the entire organization's growth.

Think about learning to drive. In most places, a person must pass a written exam to get a learner's permit. Beforehand, they study a manual to learn how the car works, read about how to operate the vehicle, and get a sense of the rules of the road. But a person who aces this test isn't guaranteed to be a good driver, and they aren't simply granted a license—they must also practice driving under the watchful eye of an adult driver who observes them and provides important real-time feedback.

The same is true in business—learning and training are valuable, but most meaningful growth occurs through real-world practice, mistakes, and feedback.

To keep your employees on a high-growth trajectory, you have to give them space to make mistakes and help them identify areas of improvement. Even the most talented employees have deficiencies, and these are often trapped in people's blind spots, which is why they need them brought to their attention in a direct but respectful way.

I would go as far as to argue that the ability to take feedback well is also a virtue that should be sought out. At Scribe Media, a book publishing and marketing company, they teach not only how to give feedback but also how to receive it. One thing they teach is "assume feedback is about the work, never the person." This helps people who receive feedback avoid being defensive. A manager never critiques the person (e.g., "You did bad work.") but instead talks about the work they do (e.g. "This work is not up to standards. Let me explain why and how you can fix it in the future.").

Scribe Media not only coaches employees—the company teaches their clients as well. For example, during the book cover design process, they coach author clients to give specific feedback and say things like, "I do not like having blue associated with my brand. I would like to explore other colors," versus something like, "It doesn't feel right."

People who do not want to learn from their own mistakes and experiences tend to repeat them. This is why, in our hiring, we are always drawn to people who are comfortable discussing past mistakes, sharing what they've learned from them, and even responding to feedback during the interview process.

LEARNING TO GIVE FEEDBACK

Having established the importance of feedback, let's dive into how to create a culture that has a level of psychological safety that fosters feedback. Building psychological safety takes time, is a top-down exercise, and often emanates from having a healthy culture in place already.

Psychological safety is, by nature, tied directly to an absence of fear within an organization. A psychologically safe environment is one where employees are not afraid to make mistakes, report problems, or ask questions without fear of retribution. We'll dig into building psychological safety in an organization more deeply in the emotional capacity chapter, but it's important context for enabling feedback.

Many leaders make the mistake of creating a culture that discourages the sharing of mistakes or errors. They can do this directly by making an example of people who make mistakes or challenge leadership or indirectly by ignoring feedback and discouraging candor. Rather than eliminating mistakes, all these leaders are doing is ensuring that when mistakes do occur—and they always do, even with the most talented, conscientious employees—they will go unreported. No one learns from mistakes that have been swept under the rug, and there often isn't an opportunity to rectify them. This is a terrible outcome for an organization's employees, culture, and bottom line.

We expect that people are going to make mistakes. What we don't want is for people to repeat the same mistakes because they haven't internalized the learning, shared it with others, or made a change to a system or process that might prevent the mistake in the future. We've made it a policy that managers complete a debrief form to share with their team when we lose a client or make a major mistake. The form author is instructed to answer several questions modeled after the military technique of an after-action review:

▸ Please describe the incident.
▸ What was the impact?
▸ What went right? What went wrong?
▸ How could we have better anticipated this outcome?
▸ If applicable, how did we try to rectify or solve the situation?

- ▸ What was the outcome and/or next steps?
- ▸ What can we learn for next time?
- ▸ What other departments need to be involved/notified?

These reports don't take long to complete, and they ensure that key learnings from mistakes are preserved for future knowledge and growth.

Once mistakes are normalized and discussed, the next step is to ensure leaders and managers respond to those issues in a productive way.

First and foremost, feedback in an organization should not come in the form of personal or character attacks. Feedback should be focused on the behavior or actions of an employee, never on their fixed character traits—this is what Scribe Media emphasizes strongly, as shared earlier.

For example, the feedback many managers find themselves giving at some point in their career is that they don't believe a direct report is incorporating enough strategic thinking into their work.

As with most feedback examples, there are two ways to deliver this coaching, and you'll probably see immediately which one is the better choice:

- ▸ **Option A:** A manager sits down with an employee and

tells them they are not a strategic thinker and they need to improve in this area to advance in the company. The manager thinks they're delivering helpful, if blunt, feedback, but the direct report feels attacked, hurt, and unsure if it's actually something they can change and how to go about doing so.

▸ **Option B:** A manager sits down with an employee and points to specific examples of where the employee's work was not strategic enough and why it generated a poor outcome. The manager is careful to avoid characterizing the employee as nonstrategic—instead, the feedback is entirely situational. Even better, the manager helps the employee brainstorm how they could've been more strategic and give specific examples. The employee leaves the meeting with an understanding of where they've fallen short and should be motivated to address similar situations differently going forward.

The reality is that it's possible the person really is not strategic enough for the role. But that conclusion should only be reached once the person's work repeatedly does not meet the required strategic threshold after they've been coached to improve. If feedback is about improvement, telling someone they don't have a required characteristic won't lead to improvement; it's more likely to lead to demoralization or disengagement.

Feedback should always be situational, not personal. Similarly, while it can be fine to tell someone that something they did was not a wise choice, it does real and long-lasting harm if you tell someone they are stupid, incompetent, or incapable as a person.

I have spoken with so many employees whose confidence is still badly damaged years later as a result of a boss who criticized their character or personally insulted them. It doesn't make them want to improve. Instead, it makes them quit or, even worse, decide to quit mentally and then stay until they find a new job.

It helps to have a framework that you can train around for giving feedback. A tried-and-true one is the SBO framework of feedback, which is built on three key pillars:

▶ **Situation:** Describe the context of the scenario the employee was in.

▶ **Behavior:** Describe what happened or what was observed, being careful not to assume you know their intent at the time.

▶ **Outcome:** Explain the impact of the employee's behavior, why it was an issue, and most importantly why it is bad for them. Finally, the focus should be on how they can improve their approach in the future to achieve better results.

The beauty of the SBO framework is it removes character criticisms from the conversation. You aren't critiquing a person's personality or aptitude—you are reviewing their actions in a certain context, explaining why those actions didn't get the best outcome, and discussing how to improve for next time. Instead of leaving the person feeling attacked, you're ostensibly helping them on the road to improvement.

To see the SBO framework in practice, consider the following scenario. An employee, Simon, has a monthly report due to a client at the end of the week. Unfortunately, the week really gets away from Simon. By Wednesday, he begins worrying he can't get the report done in time, but rather than informing his manager, Catherine, and asking for help or guidance, he ignores the issue and hopes for the best.

By the time Friday afternoon arrives, Simon realizes there is no chance he'll be able to deliver the report. Just before close of business, he writes an apologetic email to the client informing them that the report is not done and that it will be delivered next week. Simon also copies Catherine on the email. This is the first time Catherine is made aware of the issue—after it is too late to intervene or fix it.

Put yourself in Catherine's shoes: how would you feel? You'd likely feel embarrassed to be learning of this problem at the same time as the client, frustrated with Simon for failing to manage his time properly, and even more disappointed that he neglected to reach out for help earlier.

Put in this situation, a lot of managers would tell Simon how disappointed they are, let him know that this type of mistake cannot happen again, and say that it makes them question whether they can count on him at all. But as an experienced manager, Catherine knows directing her frustration at Simon in this way won't make things better or lead to improvement in the future.

Instead, here's what Catherine says at her one-on-one check-in with Simon the next Monday, following the SBO framework.

▶ **Situation:** *As I understand it, you were having an unusually busy week, and it became clear as the week went on that you were unlikely to complete the monthly report for our client. I'll also note this monthly report is something that we always prioritize getting done on time, as it offers crucial information for our client and helps us maintain trust with them.*

▶ **Behavior:** *When Friday arrived, you realized there wouldn't be time to get the report done. So you informed the client, apologized for the delay, and copied me to keep me in the loop*

▶ **Outcome:** *The issue is that our client has come to expect these reports on time. They rely on this data to evaluate our performance and determine next month's budget that we manage on* *their behalf. When these reports aren't delivered on time, it can impact both their confidence in our work and our revenue, especially when they discover at the last minute that they won't be receiving the report. It also negatively impacts the level of trust you have with your team manager, who relied on you to complete this report on time and now will be more likely to look over your shoulder. I believe there are several things we can do in the future to handle a situation like this better for everyone involved, including you.*

First, this monthly report should be at the top of your priority list at the beginning of the month. When you plan out your schedule it should be built around getting it done, even if it means putting other work aside. If you ever need help rearranging your priorities, please let me know as soon as possible—I can help you. Finally, when you realize you might not be able to complete a client deliverable like this, please let me know as soon as you realize it may be at risk. I will either help you get it done in time or work with you to inform the client in a timely, effective way that minimizes their frustration and disruption to the budget. Clients don't like hearing that deliverables won't get done, but they'd rather hear about it as far in advance of the deadline as possible so they don't feel blindsided. Are we clear on how this can be better managed if it happens again in the future?

In this example, Catherine avoids criticizing Simon personally while still being direct and holding him accountable. She explains why Simon made a poor choice in that specific situation and how it impacted both the business and Catherine personally, and she gives clear steps Simon can take if he encounters a similar situation in the future. Simon is aware of his mistake and knows he has to improve, but rather than feeling attacked and isolated, he leaves the one-on-one with his manager's support and a clear plan to do better next time.

While the framework used to deliver feedback is crucial, the way a leader broaches the issue in a feedback conversation is just as important. In this case, too many leaders take an indirect approach to avoid putting the feedback recipient on the defensive or to spare themselves some discomfort by easing into the conversation.

A favorite fallback for many leaders is the compliment sandwich, which often goes by the less tactful name of shit sandwich. A compliment sandwich is when someone opens a feedback conversation by telling someone what they are doing well. This is a way to soften the blow and establish a good rapport with the person. Then they'll give the constructive or difficult feedback, which is really the purpose of the conversation. Finally, the person ends the conversation with more compliments or positive feedback, hoping to end on a high note.

The compliment sandwich is a terrible approach. While it's certainly fine to give balanced feedback, it's best not to wrap it in this way. It leaves the person who is receiving the feedback either confused, unaware of the importance of the constructive feedback, or having that unpleasant feeling of being treated with kid gloves.

In the classic movie 1992 movie "A Few Good Men," a senior military leader named Colonel Nathan Jessup—played famously by Jack Nicholson—responds angrily to criticism of his leadership decisions during a court trial by shouting one of the most famous movie lines of all time.

"You can't handle the truth!"

While the line is often repeated, I could not disagree more; I believe people **can** handle the truth.

I've found people prefer the truth, especially when it is delivered in a direct but respectful and appropriate way—not sandwiched between half-hearted compliments.

Not only do I advocate against the compliment sandwich, but I have learned from both our difficult conversation training sessions and from real-world experience that it's best for both parties to get straight to the point and avoid dancing around the issue at hand, as our participants quickly learn. It may help to try one of these openings that gets right to the heart of the matter:

▶ "Just to be up front, this is going to be a difficult conversation."

▶ "I need to share some feedback that I think will help you improve."

▶ "What I'm about to say may not be easy to hear, but it's important."

Feedback is a part of learning, and you can't have a high-growth organization without it, which often involves direct, difficult, or uncomfortable conversations. Training your managers and leaders to successfully have these conversations makes a huge difference in building collective intellectual capacity.

LEARNING TO RECEIVE FEEDBACK

It's not uncommon for a reader to disagree with something I wrote, but it is rarer for such a response to come from within our company walls. However, this was the case when an AP employee was upset by something I wrote in one of my weekly Friday Forward posts.

I first heard about this employee's reaction from a more senior person in the organization who had been approached by the junior employee to discuss it. Even though Friday Forward isn't related to our business and it was not a workplace issue, the senior employee reached out to me to let me know about the junior employee's reaction, as it had been discussed with several people by that point. I thanked the senior employee for letting me know and strongly encouraged her to ask the junior employee to reach out to me directly to discuss their feedback, as I am always open to feedback and want to make people comfortable engaging with leadership.

The employee did reach out, and we scheduled a one-on-one conversation over Zoom about what I had written. I began by hearing them out and thanking them for the feedback. Then we delved into an interesting conversation about the Friday Forward post.

As it turned out, the root of the issue was that the employee interpreted something I wrote in a way that was very different from what I intended. We had an open conversation about whether intent matters most in these situations or if the audience's reaction or interpretation is more relevant. We both had different viewpoints and each shared examples that I believe impacted the other's thinking in a positive and productive way.

I ended the discussion by thanking the employee again for reaching out, and I invited them to feel free to come to me directly if they had a similar issue or concern in the future. Since that conversation, I've been more conscious about paying attention to the words I choose in my writing, especially if they seem susceptible to multiple interpretations. I still say what I mean and don't need everyone to agree with what I say, but I have gotten better at identifying words that may create confusion or ambiguity.

I've always tried to model an open-door policy at the company—I want employees to be able to come to me and other leaders if they have an issue or concern, partly to be a more accessible leader but especially to reinforce our culture of feedback. Though this example wasn't directly related to the company, I still felt it was an important demonstration of that policy and hoped the employee would share the experience with others so they felt comfortable doing the same.

Training leaders and managers to give feedback effectively only works if employees are also trained to receive it well. It's obviously easier for people to take feedback when it's described in the ways outlined earlier—respectfully, without character attacks or judgment. But even if we aren't easily insulted or offended, no one likes having their flaws or mistakes called out. Nor are most humans predisposed to take feedback with a smile and a thank you. It's easier in the moment to ignore feedback or dismiss it as unfair.

Here's a reality check: in my experience, when people are upset about something, they are going to either tell you directly or they'll tell everyone else behind your back. Ignorance isn't bliss. This is why receiving feedback well is a skill that must be actively taught and practiced.

A large part of teaching employees to accept feedback comes from the organization's culture. If you follow the steps explained in the previous section, you'll normalize giving and getting feedback as a necessary step to growth, not a shameful experience. This is a big reason why we make sure all our leaders use the open-door policy referenced a moment ago—if an organization's leadership demonstrates that they are open to receiving feedback, people throughout the company are much more likely to follow that example.

Beyond that cultural element, however, there are also specific things we coach our team to do in the moment when receiving feedback.

▸ **Listen and don't be defensive.** If a person makes a big show about opening themselves up to feedback but then interrupts or acts defensive as they receive the feedback, they are demonstrating that they are not really open to learning. Let the person finish speaking before you say anything, other than to ask clarifying questions.

▸ **Don't focus on your response.** When someone gives you feedback, don't start building your response in your head as they are talking. Doing this will prevent you from fully hearing and processing the feedback you're getting, and people can often tell when you aren't really listening. Instead, you can respond later, ideally after you have had time to reflect.

▸ **Respond first with thank you.** If a person is giving you feedback in good faith, always say thank you and be appreciative at the start of your response. It takes courage to give professional feedback, especially to leadership. By expressing gratitude in the moment, you reinforce to them that you value what they have to say and encourage them to take a similar approach in getting feedback themselves.

You won't always agree with the feedback you receive, nor do you always have to act on it. But even in those cases, it's best to respond according to these guidelines to ensure you keep the doors of communication open. Otherwise, it will likely be the last time that person gives you any feedback directly; they will just share it with someone else behind your back.

For many people, receiving feedback is just as difficult as giving it, if not harder. But building intellectual capacity in an organization requires both sides of a feedback conversation to be fully engaged, effective, and respectful.

System Upgrade

Investing in your team's intellectual capacity is a great example of incentive alignment from a talent development standpoint. The best talent in the market today wants to learn, and businesses want their employees to consistently improve—ideally at the rate that the organization needs them to grow to and fill the ranks of leadership.

Cultures that build intellectual capacity in the ways shared in this chapter have three key advantages:

1. They do better work, because they have a workforce of people who have the knowledge and processes to be exceptional at what they do.
2. They work more efficiently, because they are better at managing time, attacking their priorities, and devoting energy toward the actions that accomplish their goals, informed by best practices. This, in turn, leads to less burnout and busywork, which we will discuss more in the next chapter.
3. They keep employees satiated by ensuring they're always learning at a pace that challenges them. An organization with high intellectual capacity can promise their employees that they'll never feel bored or stagnant and will deliver on that promise. This also drives innovation and organizational change that leaves the company better prepared for the future.

Cultivating intellectual capacity is one of the best levers companies have to drive the pace of innovation. If you build a culture where your employees are coached to improve and are given the tools and financial resources to make those improvements, the organization will continually rise to meet the opportunities and challenges of tomorrow.

ACTION STEPS

Understanding and Applying the S-Curve Concept

▸ Check out Whitney Johnson's book *Smart Growth* for a comprehensive understanding of the S-curve and what it means for leaders and organizations.

Open-Book Management Practices

▸ To learn more about open-book management with company finances, check out Bo Burlingham and Jack Stack's organization, The Great Game of Business. They have tons of insights and I've benefited personally from many of them. Their page is linked at **robertglazer.com/eyt-resources**.

Creating a Learning Culture

▸ Start a Book Club or Podcast Club for your team or organization.

▸ See the list of book recommendations for Capacity Building, linked at **robertglazer.com/eyt-resources**.

▸ Check out the Better Book Club, a great resource for starting a club at your organization, linked at **robertglazer.com/eyt-resources**.

Giving and Receiving Feedback

▸ Read *Principles* by Ray Dalio for a detailed overview of a culture driven by psychological safety and transparency.

▸ Read *Radical Candor* by Kim Scott for a great framework for delivering and receiving feedback—and a lot of great insights about management in general. Also, check out my interview with Kim on the Elevate Podcast, linked at **robertglazer.com /eyt-resources**.

Chapter Four

BUILD YOUR TEAM'S PHYSICAL CAPACITY

*"Sometimes, the greatest gift you can give
your team is to let them go home."*

—Kim Scott

In 2017, Marissa Mayer exited as CEO of Yahoo under significant pressure and scrutiny. Mayer's tenure was marred by a string of failed acquisitions and an investigation into an unreported hack that led to the compromise of user data.

This was not the outcome most people expected when Mayer took the reins as CEO in 2012 to great fanfare after a storied thirteen-year career at Google. Mayer had started as Google's twentieth employee, led development efforts of key company products such as Google Search and Google Maps, and exited the company as a fast-rising star.

During Mayer's meteoric rise at Google, she was known for her extreme devotion to her work. In particular, she would reference pulling frequent all-nighters and had discussed a 130-hour workweek as a point of pride in several interviews.

Clearly Mayer was a success at Google with this approach, so what went wrong at Yahoo? In retrospect, there were some pretty noticeable clues that Mayer was building the type of culture that rewarded working hard rather than working smart.

In her first year at Yahoo, Mayer caused a bit of a controversy both inside and outside the company when she gave birth to her first child, a son, in her first few months on the job and returned to work just two weeks later. She even set up a nursery next to her office.

Two years later, the pattern repeated itself: Mayer gave birth to twin daughters and returned to work after only a few weeks of leave, with reporters sharing that Mayer was working from her hospital bed shortly after her girls were born. All the while, she continued to trumpet the virtues of her nonstop work ethos.[i]

While Mayer's dedication to her job might seem admirable, it's illuminating to do some quick math on what a 130-hour workweek looks like in reality. In a five-day workweek, 130 hours would amount to 26 hours a day, so obviously Mayer was putting in serious time on her weekends as well. However, even if Mayer worked seven days per week, a 130-hour workweek would mean averaging over 18 hours daily. That leaves less than six hours per day for sleeping, eating, personal maintenance, and, well, life.

This behavior is neither healthy nor sustainable; maintaining this work schedule over the long term seems like a great recipe for extreme isolation, a nervous breakdown, or a heart attack—whichever comes first.

Furthermore, what kind of example does a leader with this type of punishing schedule set for their employees? A leader sets the tone for the entire company, and an executive's work style or schedule is often seen as the benchmark.

Mayer's extreme schedule epitomizes a workaholic style that was valorized during the past two decades. This was especially true in Silicon Valley and the United States, much to the chagrin of our friends in Europe, who we often belittled for their notable separation between work and life. As prominent American executives boasted about their minimal sleeping habits and lack of vacations, their approach became a dominant professional standard of high-growth companies, based on the assumption that more working hours lead to better outcomes.

However, this playbook clearly didn't work for Yahoo. Furthermore, it has become increasingly clear that this type of behavior and culture takes a personal and professional toll and causes organizations to burn through talent quickly.

Fortunately, many leaders today have learned that sacrificing health, sleep, and overall wellness doesn't get the best outcomes in the long term. After the COVID-19 pandemic, many employees have made it clear that they are no longer interested in this sort of 24/7 work or hustle culture, and they won't work for leaders or companies who embrace and celebrate it.

With respect to sleep, there's also real science that pushing employees to the brink of sleep deprivation is simply bad business. A popular study on sleep and work found that a person who sleeps less than five hours a night is as cognitively impaired as someone who is legally drunk.[ii] Marissa Mayer wouldn't hire someone who showed up to work drunk each day, but her leadership example effectively encouraged the same behavior.

In contrast to Mayer, however, it's heartening to see more leaders today talk openly about protecting their sleep schedules.[iii] Two of the most well-known examples of this are Warren Buffett and Jeff Bezos, who both claim to sleep eight hours per night.[iv] These leaders certainly have enough work responsibilities to justify regular all-nighters as well, but they choose not to go that route because they have seen how it hampers their performance.

The data also supports these evolving viewpoints. Researchers are sounding alarm bells that we need more sleep. The National Sleep Foundation found that the average adult needs seven to nine hours of sleep per night to perform well cognitively.[v]

Picture a person who barely gets five hours of sleep per night, mainlines sugar and caffeine for energy, never takes breaks to recharge throughout the day or the year, and neglects self-care activities such as meditation or exercise. Would you expect this person to show up to work well rested, with a clear head and a high level of energy? Would you expect them to be able to make sound decisions under pressure? And even if they could, is there any reason to believe they could sustain this long term without eventually hitting a wall?

The answer is clearly no. And this brings us to the crucial third element of capacity building: **physical capacity**.

Physical capacity relates to your health, well-being, and physical performance. In a professional setting, people with high physical capacity show up energized and focused each day, stay effective in stressful situations, and prioritize staying in balance. People who combine physical capacity with the intellectual capacity improvements detailed in the previous chapter get more done in less time, allowing them to step away from work at the end of each day.

In turn, they can devote more time and energy to things that are important outside work, which keeps them healthier and more balanced overall. This is another instance where capacity building creates a virtuous cycle.

Our brains and bodies depend on each other. Employees and leaders who prioritize their well-being and energy tend to perform better in all aspects of their life, especially at work. Leaders who help their employees build their physical capacity will get better long-term performance and employee retention.

The best leaders and companies today want their employees to prioritize their physical and mental health; they want employees who work smarter, not longer.

Although it may seem counterintuitive, these leaders are the ones who attract and retain top talent at their organizations. The result is a high-performing team that produces top results, doesn't experience burnout, feels their workplace cares about them as people, and stays together for the long haul.

Building Buffers

It's easy to see how people can exhaust themselves working at a high-performing organization. Some employees work extremely long hours to gain favor with leaders, then sacrifice sleep to carve out time for themselves. Others make themselves constantly available for work needs and messages and find themselves unable to wind down at the end of the day as a result. Everyone who has answered emails right before bed knows that some messages, or their proposed replies, will replay in their head all night, keeping them from settling into restful sleep.

This phenomenon has often been exacerbated by the recent shift to remote and hybrid work that has removed the last remaining physical barriers between work and home life. This makes it much harder for employees to unwind and recover from the workday and prevents them from getting the sleep we *know* is crucial to cognitive performance. The data shows people working from home do more, not less. The Society for Human Resource Management (SHRM) found that 70 percent of workers who transitioned to remote work during the pandemic began working on weekends, and 45 percent put in more hours during the workweek as well.[vi] Remote workers save time and energy by avoiding a commute, but they often end up investing that time back into their work without the right boundaries.

Leaders should want their employees to show up for work well rested and cognitively sharp. A workforce of exhausted people won't perform at a high level over a sustained interval. If anything, these workaholic zombies will stumble through the workday cognitively impaired, make mistakes, and struggle to get even the most basic tasks done correctly the first time, which leads to even less sleep and creates a vicious cycle.

The best way for leaders to get rested, energized employees in their workplace is to help their teams create and sustain boundaries between work and home life. There are a few best practices that accomplish this:

► **Don't brag about hero hours.** As is often the case, the model you provide as a leader sets the bar for your team's behavior. If you brag about working fourteen hours a day and on weekends, then your team is likely to emulate your behavior to keep up with you. They will believe that working beyond the workday is the best way to earn your approval and will do so accordingly, even if you don't explicitly ask them to. Mayer may have communicated to working moms at Yahoo that she did not expect them to follow her own maternity leave schedule, but it's hard to believe that her example did not define her employees' expectations in some way. "Do as I say, not as I do" rarely works for parents or leaders.

► **Take time to unplug.** I cannot tell you how many leaders I've met who have convinced themselves their leadership duties are too important for them to take a vacation and disconnect from work, going years without a true break. If you make a fully offline, relaxing vacation seem like a sign of weakness, that's how your leaders will behave, both individually and with their teams. You are also much more likely to eventually hit a wall and experience burnout.

▸ **Limit off-hour communication.** Many leaders make it clear they don't expect responses to their late-night emails, but an employee still might feel pressure to respond, especially if they are more junior in the organization. Personally, I like to clean out my email on a Saturday morning when I'm free of distractions and can focus, but I've realized over time that doing so sets an implicit pressure for people to respond over the weekend. A best practice I adopted years ago is to use the delayed delivery function when sending nonurgent emails outside the regular workweek. This way, I can send an email on the weekend when it is easiest for me, but the recipient doesn't get it until around 8:00 a.m. the next business day.

▸ **Set clear deadlines.** When giving a task or request to a member of your team, it's always helpful to set a deadline for when you need it to be completed. I've had plenty of experiences where I've assigned something to a member of my team that wasn't urgent, only to have them frantically rearrange their schedule to do it for me ASAP or assume they needed to worknights and weekends to get it done. Without clear deadlines, employees tend to think everything they are asked to do is urgent and important. Help them prioritize by setting better expectations up front.

To model healthy work-life integration, talk openly and give employees permission to create boundaries between work and home life. Nowhere is this more important than with communication; if you regularly emphasize the points above in your communication, your people will notice that you care about protecting their time outside work. They won't feel a need to work extreme hours to earn your respect and may actually accomplish more when they are working.

With that said, it's important *not* to set the expectation that employees will never have to put in extra hours, especially at high-growth organizations. No matter how dedicated a leader is to work-life buffers, there are going to be times when an extra level of effort and off-hour communications are necessary, especially to prepare for a big sales pitch or product launch or to finalize a crucial project with a tight deadline.

If employees want flexibility during work hours for things that come up in their personal lives, they need to understand the same will also be required on occasion from their work obligations—it can't be a one-way street. They key is to make these the exceptions and not the rule.

It's also important to set the tone early by making buffer setting a significant part of employee onboarding. Think about the last time you started a new job: you no doubt felt pressure to prove yourself and establish your work ethic. Because of this, new employees can fall into poor work-life integration habits that stick for their entire time at a company.

Organizations and leaders should outline expectations for a normal workday for new employees, encourage them to disconnect outside work hours, and clarify that long hours aren't the path to recognition and rewards. What's most important is getting the right outcomes and results.

Here are a few more practical tactics companies can use to model and incentivize healthy buffers between work and life:

▸ **Incentivize desired behavior.** Consider offering a vacation bonus. We've instituted a policy where employees who take a week's vacation and unplug from work while they're off can use a percentage of their wellness stipend for the year toward the vacation. This demonstrates that we want employees to take time off, and it makes it even easier to justify a vacation—that money can go a long way toward planning a vacation that lets you get away mentally and physically. It also has the added benefit of encouraging more forethought about delegation before the vacation and not making any one person the single point of contact or failure. If everything goes through a single person, there is usually no way to truly detach, and it also concentrates risk for the company.

- **Emphasize physical separation.** Encourage any team members who work remotely to physically separate their workspace in their home. If an employee's "office" is a desk in the corner of their bedroom, they may feel like they're sleeping at the office, not working from home. It helps to set aside a budget to support getting people set up to work from home properly and productively.
- **Show, don't tell.** Make it clear that the company's leaders prioritize their own self-care and interests outside work. Share your personal accomplishments and demonstrate that you take time to recharge and unplug and take real vacations. For example, while on vacation, you might set up your internal auto reply to say something like "I'm really making an effort to be offline during my time off, but I'll handle this when I return on Monday." Remember that when you're a leader, your personal choices quickly become unofficial guidelines that your team members follow.

Here's the reality: people need to have a life outside work in order to feel fully motivated and energized during the workday. Even if employees aren't especially passionate about their work, they'll be invested in excelling at it if they see their work as helping to enable their fulfilling personal life. Constantly working long hours on things that are unimportant is more likely to lead to resentment and subpar performance than better outcomes.

The truth is that many high-performing organizations see little need to track or focus on their employees' hours because they have better means of evaluating performance.

Managing Outcomes, Not Hours

Which of these two salespeople would you rather hire?

- ▸ **Salesperson A**, who works sixty hours a week and closes $2 million in business per year.
- ▸ **Salesperson B**, who works thirty hours a week and closes $3 million in business per year.

This isn't a trick. Anyone should prefer the salesperson who closes 50 percent more business per year, regardless of how many hours they work. While Salesperson A is clearly willing to make a lot of calls, Salesperson B gets better results by focusing on the activities that drive a better outcome for *both themselves and the company.*

Most sales leaders evaluate their employees based on outcomes, but their colleagues who lead other parts of the organization often don't do the same because their most crucial metrics are often less obvious and harder to design. But following this practice—defining the outcomes that are most important and holding employees accountable to them—you can move the culture away from a focus on inputs and hours.

Not only does managing to outcomes get employees focused on the right things, but it can also improve physical capacity. Most crucially, it will help you identify places where you have a lose-lose value proposition: employees working exhausting hours who are unlikely to achieve the desired outcome anyway. In many cases, what's needed is either a better clarification of what is most important or a change in the person responsible for those outcomes, not more laps on the hamster wheel.

Working long hours poses an occupational health risk that kills hundreds of thousands of people each year, according to a landmark study by the World Health Organization released in 2021.[vii]

That study found that people working 55 or more hours each week face an estimated 35 percent higher risk of a stroke and a 17 percent higher risk of dying from heart disease, compared to people following the widely accepted standard of working 35 to 40 hours in a week. The study also found that in 2016, 488 million people were exposed to the risks of working long hours and more than 745,000 people died that year from overwork-related strokes and heart disease.

If that data isn't convincing enough, here's another reason

to move your culture away from an input focus: the math simply disproves the idea that working more hours translates into getting better results. While some managers value long hours and face time, these factors don't guarantee great performance. In fact, sometimes employees can use face time to cover for a lack of actual results— and leaders can overlook an underperformer who is always working, because they are mistaking busyness for productivity.

To understand why, consider the Pareto principle. This concept, also known as the 80/20 rule, was named after esteemed economist Vilfredo Pareto. He showed that 80 percent of consequences come from 20 percent of all actions, illustrating an unequal relationship between inputs and outputs. Consider these examples:

► In general, 80 percent of our sales come from 20 percent of our clients. This means the inverse is also true, and the majority of clients deliver a comparatively small amount of revenue and profit. However, we spend 80 percent of our time on those relationships.

► We wear 20 percent of our clothes 80 percent of the time. This means all that clutter in your closet mostly comes from clothes you wear rarely, if ever.

The Pareto principle highlights the fact that most employees spend 80 percent of their time on things that are comparatively inessential to the organization's success. Even if your employees are constantly working during their long hours, they will spend much of that time on things that fundamentally don't move the business forward—monitoring email, doing busywork, or attending inefficient and unnecessary meetings.

Perhaps this is why many companies have begun experimenting with four-day workweeks. These organizations are betting that employees can get as much done in four days as they do in five by simply spending more time on the right priorities and by eliminating unnecessary work and meetings.

The best thing leaders can do for their employees and their organizations is setting clear professional outcomes for their teams, helping them dedicate their time toward hitting those outcomes, and measuring their people against those outcomes.

A key step in this process to shifting to outcome-based management is creating an organizational scorecard that includes the key goals, metrics, and deliverables for your organization each year by quarter. Having these scorecards is the best way to ensure your entire team knows what the business is aiming for and how they can help drive toward those goals on their teams and in their roles. Then leaders can work with their teams to set and manage outcomes that build toward the key levers in the company's scorecard.

As mentioned above, very few departments outside sales do a good job of managing to outcomes. Part of the reason is that sales has very objective metrics, but that doesn't mean you can't build similar metrics across other functions that have the same impact.

For example, imagine you want your managers to focus on developing the next generation of leaders at your company. Below are examples of an input-driven goal and an outcome-driven metric:

► **Input-driven goal:** Spend time each week thinking strategically about leadership development.

► **Outcome-driven metric:** Identify three people in your team/department this quarter who could potentially develop into your successor. Present these three names to your manager, and ensure each one has a concrete two-year personal development plan filed with HR.

While the first will ensure leaders remember to think about leadership development, the second will produce a specific list of potential leaders the organization can train and develop and is measurable. Getting the outcome that makes progress toward the organizational objective of developing future leaders is more valuable than simply allocating time toward the initiative.

Here's another example of what an outcome-oriented scorecard would look like for a manager in a customer service role:

- **Input-driven goal:** Keep customers happy.
- **Outcome-driven metrics:** 95 percent of client issues resolved without escalation to director; 90 percent of clients in portfolio meeting are exceeding their quarterly objectives; 75 percent client retention rate; and a 52-plus client net promoter score.

In this example, employees and managers are clear about what good performance looks like and success is based on the outcome achieved, not the hours spent.

If you or your team are struggling with developing outcome-driven metrics for roles outside sales, it might help to answer these key questions:

- What does success in this role look like from a metrics/output standpoint?
- What company goals or metrics is this person responsible for owning or contributing toward? For example, your sales leader should own your company's revenue goal, and the sales team should each have an outcome that builds toward that total goal.
- What does the best person/people you have in this role do exceptionally well? What is their superpower?
- If you were going away for the quarter to a deserted island and could only assign three priorities to this role to know it

was on track, what would they be? What would objectively indicate success or failure in each area when you returned?

▶ What other objective metrics can be used to evaluate a person's performance in this role? Remember, these shouldn't be input-driven, such as sales calls made or candidates interviewed. They should be outcome-driven, like sales booked or employees onboarded.

Answers to these questions will guide you to a clear set of outcomes that can form the basis of an individual scorecard and focus employees on achieving those outcomes. To make this explicit, here are outcome-driven examples you could consider for each of the major departments in an organization:

▶ **Marketing:** The number of qualified leads delivered to the sales team.

▶ **Sales:** The amount of sales booked, in dollars, or revenue delivered versus goal.

▶ **HR:** The number of employees hired or onboarded relative to the company's hiring plan, unwanted turnover rate, or the employee net promoter score.

▶ **Client Services:** A customer satisfaction or net promoter score, defined client outcomes, or the number of issues that required escalation.

▸ **Finance:** The amount of revenue and profit accrued, cash generated, average outstanding receivables and deliverables, or other important financial metrics.

▸ **Product Development:** New or improved products delivered on time, according to spec, and within budget.

Once the outcomes are made clear, your next step as a leader is to help your team prioritize those outcomes and eliminate unnecessary work. This is where it can be useful to take a minimalist approach: help employees determine the few priorities each quarter that contribute to the organization meeting its objectives and put the majority of their energy toward getting those done first. There is a lot of science that shows the ideal number of goals to have at any one time for an organization, individual, or team is three.

Rather than pushing their teams to work more, great leaders help their people maximize the portion of their workday that they spend on achieving their most important outcomes. Doing this not only helps the business grow, but it helps employees work fewer hours—and be less stressed and exhausted—while still feeling like they've accomplished what they must for the company to succeed.

On top of it, people tend to be more energized when they get important things done, see the clear connection to departmental and organizational goals, and are part of a team where everyone is rowing in the same direction. A leader's responsibility is to help make those connections clear.

Prioritizing Health

In some ways, physical capacity is the most difficult capacity to build on a professional team. After all, health is a highly personal topic and can be sensitive for many people.

Still, helping your employees prioritize their personal health and wellness is valuable, for both the employees and the company. Though people can separate their personal and professional lives, they are still the same person in both areas of life, and things like stress, fatigue, and a lack of energy in one area inevitably spill over into the other, with measurable consequences for both spheres.

A Deloitte study found that 77 percent of employees have experienced burnout at their current job.[viii] Statistically, there is a very good chance some of these employees work on your team. A key driver of burnout is an inability to prioritize self-care and maintain healthy habits. The bigger a burden work is in a person's life, the less likely they are to take care of themselves. And while you can't and shouldn't monitor what your employees eat or require them to exercise, you can create a culture that both makes it easier for them to prioritize their health without being heavy-handed.

One way to help employees build physical capacity is to create company initiatives that encourage wellness. One of my favorite things we've done on this front is a Wellness Challenge to help our team manage pandemic stress. We collected names of everyone who wanted to participate and divided them into teams. Then we challenged every person to do something each workday to improve their wellness. Each day a person did a wellness activity was worth one point, and teams competed to see who could earn the most points over the course of six weeks.

The challenge was designed to be inclusive and accessible to all fitness levels. To earn a point, employees could go for a run, lift weights, take a leisurely walk, do yoga, or even meditate for a few minutes. We weren't pushing everyone in our company to train for a marathon—we were simply encouraging them to make small investments in their self-care each day, *during the workday*. This demonstrated that leadership cared about their personal wellness and wanted them to take time for their wellness during what would otherwise be considered regular business hours.

In addition to encouraging employee wellness, the challenge was also a bonding experience for our team. Everyone from our entry-level employees to our executives participated in playful trash talk on our Wellness Challenge Slack channel.

This Wellness Challenge is a group-tactic way to encourage wellness, but companies can also do this by encouraging individual actions that build physical capacity. First, encourage your employees to lean into the boundaries between work and life and build flexibility into their schedules. You can't expect your employees to prioritize wellness if you don't give them time to do it, just as you wouldn't force someone to sit on the couch all day and be surprised when they can't run a marathon.

Give your employees the freedom and flexibility to set a schedule that suits their lifestyle and their self-care. If you have an employee who wants to fit an extended workout into their morning before they start working or end their day a bit early to go for a jog before they pick up their kids, you should be encouraging this behavior as long as they are meeting their goals and objectives and it does not impact client or customer experience. Plus, there's a performance benefit to giving your employees time to exercise—a Harvard study found exercise improves cognitive performance and memory.[ix]

Likewise, you can encourage employees to take an extended break during the workday, which can be used to hit the gym, attend a yoga class, or even just take some time to rest and recharge. As a leader, you can model this behavior in your own calendar by planning exercise into your schedule so those around you see that it is a priority and encouraged.

This is another benefit to managing employees based on their outcomes, not their time inputs. If an employee is expected to work exactly eight hours a day, they'll likely be left feeling like they can't take time for their health during the workday. But if an employee's day is focused on accomplishing the most important outcomes, they can build their schedule around getting those things done first and use whatever free time is left to take care of their health.

If you want to take it a step further, the company can explicitly help employees hit their fitness goals or motivate them to set them. The simplest way to do that is creating a wellness stipend, where each employee is allocated several hundred dollars to spend on expenses related to health and wellness. AP employees can use our wellness benefit for everything from gym memberships to exercise equipment to meditation apps to massages.

We even made wellness a core feature of one of our favorite culture programs. As part of the preparation for our annual all-company summit each year, we ask our employees on a few occasions to share personal goals they hope to achieve in the upcoming year. Not surprisingly, many of these goals are physical—we've had employees aspire to run marathons, participate in triathlons, get into CrossFit, lose weight, or even compete in a sport at a high level.

As part of our AP Dream Program, we review these submissions and pick a group of employees each year who we'll financially support to help them reach their goals. We've given employees free personal training sessions with top trainers, signed them up to work with a running coach, and gifted them meditation apps to help them master mindfulness. Some of the associated goals were meditating a certain number of days per month, completing a 10K, completing a half Ironman, or running a marathon. This Dream Program is one of my favorite culture initiatives we've created at the company and is the ultimate win-win.

Not only does this make our employees feel heard and valued, but their performance almost always improves as they build their physical capacity. We've had several of our team members see their best work coincide with training to reach a fitness goal. The increased confidence that comes with making progress toward a physical goal and the increased energy provided by better physical health create positive outcomes both inside and outside work.

The goal should never be to put pressure on your employees to be healthy. This is why it's important to make these types of wellness challenges opt-in only and not push people toward specific fitness benchmarks. Instead, developing a culture that puts a priority on health should provide the encouragement and flexibility your employees need to create their own wellness goals, with the knowledge that their company supports them in those efforts.

Giving your people the time to pursue healthy activities or incentivizing it in small ways is often all it takes to get your team on the path toward building physical capacity—and they will reap the benefits personally and professionally.

Self-Care Isn't Selfish

Each time you prepare for takeoff on an airplane, you are asked to watch a safety video where flight attendants instruct you to put on your own oxygen mask *before* assisting others.

The first time you heard this, you may have been taken aback, especially if you were traveling with a child. It's natural to assume that passengers would prioritize their loved ones' safety over their own. Some even find it painful to imagine taking time to put on their own mask while the person next to them struggles to breathe or begins panicking.

Yet helping others before putting on your own oxygen mask does much more harm than good. A parent who passes out from a lack of oxygen is a liability to their child.

This is a useful metaphor for how physical capacity aids organizations.

All successful teams—in business, sports, or otherwise—require sacrifice for the greater good. Knowing this, some leaders think they have to demand their teams' total commitment, even at the expense of their personal well-being. Likewise, some employees feel they must overextend themselves to advance in an organization.

But just as a person needs to put on their own oxygen mask before assisting others, an employee must protect their well-being to become a sustainable high performer. While an employee might accomplish a lot in the short term by sacrificing sleep, working long hours, and never taking a day off, they're virtually guaranteed to burn out in the long run. When that burnout arrives—and it always does—they are most likely to quit the company abruptly and force their already overworked teams to pick up the slack. This is a poor outcome for the employee and the company, and it induces a vicious cycle where additional strain is placed on the rest of the team.

In short, while prioritizing your self-care can feel selfish, the alternative is giving your colleagues and everyone else in your life a diminished-capacity version of yourself.

While our brains do most of the heavy lifting in knowledge work, we rely on our bodies to put in the hours at our desks. Leaders should model healthy work practices for their teams and give them the time, flexibility, and resources to take care of their own health if they want to attract and retain the best talent.

By investing in your team's physical capacity, you're creating a long-term payoff for just a bit of short-term investment. It's a pretty easy trade-off to make, especially when you consider the alternative.

Working Smarter, Not Harder

All of the above brings us back to the story of Marissa Mayer. Though Mayer's extreme work habits frequently made headlines in her early days at Yahoo, there was not much else to celebrate during her tenure as CEO, as hinted at the beginning of the chapter. Mayer exited the company in 2017 under significant pressure and hasn't held a major leadership role since.

Mayer's five-year tenure at the head of Yahoo was marked by challenges on all fronts. Yahoo experienced a collapse in employee morale and significant leadership turnover—over a third of Yahoo's workforce left the company in 2015 and 2016, and a 2016 Glassdoor survey of the company found that only 34 percent of its remaining employees expected things to improve.[x] That was before the mass layoffs started in 2016, which only made things worse.

Mayer had also embarked on an aggressive acquisition strategy, buying fifty-three companies during her tenure at a cost of over $2 billion.[xi] The majority of these acquisitions were written off as worthless. She even lost her bonus from her final two years of employment after an investigation revealed that senior Yahoo executives were aware of a major hack at the firm in 2014 but neglected to properly investigate and report it.[xii]

No one would argue that Mayer's failure at Yahoo was due to a lack of effort. However, it's not a stretch to wonder if things would have turned out differently had she focused more time on fewer strategic priorities, encouraged her team to trade one hundred–plus hour workweeks for better work-life integration, and didn't mistake working hard for working smart in the few areas that mattered most to the company's success.

This is the key lesson of physical capacity—you may believe you can sacrifice health, wellness, and sleep, especially in the professional world, but it is the leaders and teams that push themselves hard enough to diminish their well-being that often fail to achieve the ambitious goals they were working so hard to reach in the first place.

ACTION STEPS

Prioritization and Energy Management
► Read Greg McKeown's *Essentialism* for a great guide on prioritizing the most important things in work and life.

Building Buffers Between Work and Life

- ► Check out my book, *How to Thrive in the Virtual Workplace*, which offers detailed tips for building buffers between work and life and prioritizing self-care. You don't have to work remotely full time to use these tips.

Encouraging Wellness and Self-Care

- ► Start a Wellness Challenge on your own team, department, or organization. You don't even need to be a manager to do this—just bring it to your immediate manager as a suggestion and offer to set it up. Here's a simple overview of the process:
  - » Announce the Wellness Challenge and its rules to get people interested. Tell people that all they need to do is spend thirty minutes a day on some sort of wellness-oriented activity—such as jogging, yoga, playing a sport, walking, or meditating—and give a signup deadline.
  - » Once you have sign-ups for the challenge, divide the participants into teams. You can give the teams fun names—at AP, we named all our teams after animals.

» Create a form participants can use to log their progress each day. Ask them to note their name, team name, the date of the activity, and what they did. If you want, you can ask people to send picture/video proof of their activity if you don't just want to use the honor system.

» Give each team one point for each day each member of their team logs a wellness activity. So, for example, if eight members of a team log an activity on Monday, the team gets eight points.

» Create a communications channel/chat where participants can share their progress, encourage each other, and playfully compete.

» Set an end date to the Wellness Challenge. When that day comes, tally up the points and announce the winner!

Chapter Five

BUILD YOUR TEAM'S EMOTIONAL CAPACITY

*"Vulnerability is the birthplace of innovation,
creativity, and change."*

—Brené Brown

"I have never shared this part of my story before."

As I looked around the room, I saw over 150 people listening intently to every word, with many leaning in on the edges of their seats.

When the speaker finished, there was an immediate standing ovation led by people who had been openly crying just a few minutes earlier.

I have seen some of the world's most sought-after speakers,

and this speaker's command over the audience was similar. However, this was not a polished professional giving a college graduation speech or even a TED event; instead, it took place at our annual company event, AP Summit, in November 2019.

And the speaker was not one of the professional speakers who had come to inspire our team over the years. Instead, she was one of four brave employees who had volunteered to share incredibly vulnerable stories with all their colleagues in a fifteen-minute speech.

The prompt for the speaker was: **If today was your last day on earth and you could deliver a final speech to the world, what would you say?**

This is the premise of One Last Talk (OLT), a deeply personal speaking series started by world-renowned clarity coach Philip McKernan. McKernan created OLT to encourage people to speak their truth unapologetically, not only to free themselves but also to compel others to reflect on their own deep, hidden emotions.

OLT speeches are not a canned list of top five recommendations or a how-to speech. In OLT, speakers vulnerably share something they've held on to closely for most of their lives, often for the first time.

Several months before that AP Summit, I reached out to McKernan and asked if he would be willing to host an OLT at our event for employees. I thought dedicating a portion of our AP Summit to OLTs would be a powerful exercise that could model vulnerability and encourage more trust and connection among our team.

We sent out a request for four volunteers who'd be willing to go through the OLT process and work with McKernan to develop their talks. I was actually worried no one would reply, but to my surprise, we received more interest than we could accommodate and had the difficult task of selecting the speakers.

When the big day came, these four employees delivered their well-rehearsed and powerful OLTs to the entire company. By sharing something that was so intimate and personal, they displayed tremendous courage and vulnerability. Just as crucially, however, their colleagues in the audience met that vulnerability with a high degree of acceptance. Our team made the speakers feel seen, validated, and safe in sharing their very personal stories.

While these talks left the audience feeling incredibly moved and inspired, the real impact of the speeches unfolded over the next few days.

It was as if a dam had broken. Employees suddenly felt inspired to share more openly with their colleagues, completely unprompted. A pair of our employees who worked together daily for five years even shared with me that they'd learned entirely new things about each other that they wished they had known before.

The truth is, it was a bit hard to get people to stop sharing over the next few days as we shifted to different content and activities. However, the company reached a whole new level of depth and vulnerability on that day that would carry forward long past the event.

Vulnerability is a widely discussed term; by now we all know what it means and may even know why it can be valuable, especially for teamwork and leadership. But understanding vulnerability's importance is very different from building it into an organization as a practice. Doing the latter is a core part of building the final element of capacity: emotional capacity.

Emotional capacity is how you react to challenging situations, your emotional mindset, and the quality of your relationships. In an organizational context, high emotional capacity manifests itself with deep levels of trust, open lines of communications between colleagues—including on issues where there is real contention or division—and a degree of emotional resilience that allows teams to remain strong in the face of challenging situations. The result is a high level of psychological safety, which is essentially trust at scale and is essential to transparency, candor, and growth. A psychologically safe workplace is one with norms that help teams build trust readily, more quickly than they would at an average company.

Building emotional capacity might seem a bit touchy-feely for the workplace. Skeptics might say that team meetings are for problem-solving and brainstorming, not group therapy. But this misses the point and ignores the clear trend of a more integrated relationship between our lives and our work.

Emotional capacity is difficult to cultivate at a team or organizational level, and it often involves a great deal of discomfort. Our four brave volunteers who delivered their OLTs to the full company certainly felt discomfort and fear during their preparation and speeches. But their reward for pushing through those feelings was visible. Shortly after the talks, as I sat with McKernan and one of our OLT speakers who shared about their fear of a potential genetic disease that had devastated their family, I noticed a glow and sense of peacefulness about them. Surely some of this was due to getting their speech over with after all that practice, but there was also something deeper—a sense of self-reconciliation and acceptance from their colleagues that made the whole experience worthwhile.

This is the key lesson for organizations. If teams learn to push through these natural barriers of discomfort by practicing vulnerability, opening communications, creating safe discomfort, and building healthier emotional mindsets, the dividends are enormous.

Getting Real

It's fair to say there is some stigma about sharing in the workplace. In particular, many people want to avoid being seen as oversharers. However, that pendulum often swings too far in the opposite direction, leading employees to be totally closed off to their coworkers about their personal values and challenges. The result of this is a workplace where colleagues collaborate on incredibly high-leverage projects without really knowing the people they're counting on to deliver. In that vein, there can be critical things about how they communicate, show up, work, and collaborate that are unknown to themselves and their colleagues.

As stated earlier, psychological safety is foundational to all healthy organizations—it is the collection of group norms that builds trust between individuals and teams throughout the company. Psychological safety is what allows teams to have productive conflict, bring the best ideas to the surface, openly disagree, and assume that everyone on the team is rowing in the same direction. And psychological safety requires people to be comfortable with each other. Comfort requires sharing, and sharing requires vulnerability; people generally do not feel fully comfortable among others until they know them and until they make themselves known to them.

A powerful explanation of this relationship comes from a framework called the Johari window, named after its founders, psychologists Joseph Luft and Harry Ingham. It maps out awareness in two dimensions—what you know about yourself and what others know about you.[i] The four areas in the window are as follows:

▸ **Open:** What is known to you and to others.
▸ **Hidden:** What is known to you but unknown to others.
▸ **Blind Spot:** What is known to others but unknown to you.
▸ **Unknown to All:** What is unknown to you and to others.

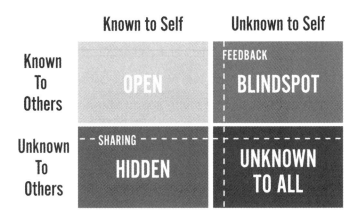

The goal with the Johari window is to expand the open square to overtake the other three quadrants—to create a more open environment where the person has improved self-awareness and has also communicated their most important needs, strengths, and weaknesses to others on the team. We expand that open quadrant in two ways.

The first way is to expand what we know—and eliminate our blind spots—by seeking out and accepting feedback, as we discussed with intellectual capacity in chapter 3.

The second way is to expand what others know—and eliminate what is hidden—through vulnerability and sharing. We'll now tackle this one.

In our chapter on spiritual capacity, we discussed the importance of self-awareness and encouraged you to have your teams find their core values, take assessments such as DiSC or CliftonStrengths, and identify their whys. This is only one step of the capacity building process as far as self-awareness is concerned. Once leaders have this awareness about themselves—what matters most to them, what behavior violates their values, what their strengths and weaknesses are—the next step is to share that knowledge with their teams, especially the people they lead. This is one of the most effective, direct ways for leaders to help their teams understand and accommodate the leader's needs.

Consider a manager who self-identifies trust as a personal core value. In my experience, that often becomes a core value because they experienced a serious violation of trust at some point in their lives, most commonly during childhood. The result is that manager often finds certain behaviors—tardiness to meetings, missed deadlines, or an ill-timed comment in a meeting—to be signs that a person cannot be trusted. These strong emotional reactions are often at a subconscious or primal level, but they lead the manager to put the offending employee in a professional penalty box.

Knowing that trust is a core value, the manager would be wise to explain the importance of trust to their team and articulate which behaviors build or reduce trust. Once they have this knowledge, members of the team can look for opportunities to engage in trust-building behaviors and better avoid the often small actions that trigger a loss of the leader's trust.

A manager who has built their spiritual capacity and knows certain behaviors violate their core values but does not share that information with their team is not going to get the best outcomes from their team or put their team members in the best position to succeed. It's like having the operating manual to a machine and not sharing it with the person who uses the machine daily.

Leaders must demonstrate vulnerability first, as the leader sets the tone for the entire team. That's why, as part of our leadership training, we don't just have our up-and-coming managers discover their values, Whys, and strengths. We also have them write out a communication plan for how they'll share these personal insights with their teams in a way that demonstrates humility, vulnerability, and self-awareness. In these plans we ask each attendee to share the following with their teams:

▸ Their list of core values
▸ Their Why Archetype, and what it means
▸ Their commitments to their team going forward
▸ Their expectations of their team going forward, based on their newfound understanding of themselves

These presentations have always had positive results in our organization. No matter what a manager's trigger points or needs may be, their teams appreciate having the information, which they can use to better manage up.

I've had to do this myself. As I shared in the spiritual capacity chapter, I constantly seek ways to improve things, almost to a fault. A good descriptor for my approach is "often pleased, never satisfied." Because of this, I am not prone to relish the view at the summit. I tend to quickly move on to the next mountain.

This approach works better for me than it does for many people on my team. I often need to remind myself that many people need to celebrate team wins or have their work recognized to feel fulfilled professionally. On many occasions, I have been guilty of not stopping to celebrate a milestone or achievement.

In other cases, I put too much focus on what can be improved versus what is working.

I have told members of my team to remind me to celebrate our wins more fully when I get caught up in the next challenge. I always appreciate when they do this so that my tendency does not become a blind spot that damages employee morale. For example, in December 2020, our company struck an important partnership with a new investor. This was at the height of the COVID-19 pandemic, so celebrating with my executive team in person was not feasible. Though I wanted to wait until we could all get together in person, I realized it was an important milestone that needed to be commemorated in the moment.

I found a company that made custom care packages and sent packages to our full executive team, then set up a Zoom call for everyone to open them and celebrate together. Team members were joined by their significant others, who had put up with months of absurd hours leading up to the deal. It wasn't the in-person celebration I had envisioned, but it was a really nice moment that everyone needed after an exhausting year with an exciting end.

This process of self-revelation isn't easy or natural for most people. Some people are very anxious about letting others see them for who they are, especially in the workplace. However, when managers take the bold step to share openly with their teams, their employees will recognize that sharing and vulnerability are assets at an organization, not detriments. In turn, they will reciprocate the behavior.

You might also consider making vulnerability or sharing a factor that is represented in your organization's core values. As mentioned earlier, one of our company core values is "Embrace Relationships," and we encourage employees to build genuine connections with clients, partners, and colleagues, not just surface-level interactions. This value draws a direct connection between vulnerability, psychological safety, and success—our team members see authenticity and vulnerability as things that drive advancement at the company.

If you're just starting to build more vulnerability into your organizational culture, you probably don't want to try something like the OLT program. However, you can build sharing and openness into your company's culture in small ways that compound over time. Here are some small steps to try:

▶ **Make personal updates part of recurring meetings.** Rather than jumping right into business, think about starting meetings by asking each member if they have any highlights they'd like to share or any challenges they've been facing outside work. A manager might even ask in a weekly team huddle, "What was the best and worst experience of your week?" All our executive team meetings begin with

ELEVATE YOUR TEAM

each member of the leadership team sharing a personal and professional highlight from the past week. Sharing these small morsels—from hitting personal goals to talking about a recent family vacation—gently pushes the boundaries of the Johari window, making it easier to talk about topics that require more trust and vulnerability. We encourage our managers to follow this same approach with their teams as well.

▸ **Use check-ins to check in.** This type of personal sharing should be a feature in one-on-one meetings as well. Managers should regularly ask their direct reports how they are doing personally to build a rapport and demonstrate they care about team members as people. This may also prompt direct reports to come to their managers with challenges and get help with obstacles they are facing, both professionally and, yes, even personally.

▸ **Encourage company-wide sharing.** Several years ago, an employee at AP started a Slack channel called "What Made Your Week" with a simple note:

"Happy Friday!!! What made your week? Did your kid say their first word or score a goal in a soccer game? Did you go on your dream vacation? Did you sign up for a marathon? Complete a lifelong goal? Big or small, share it with us! Pictures are not required but highly encouraged!"

142

The first response was from an employee who recently ran the Boston Marathon, and more submissions poured in from there, with stories of dream vacations, graduations, marriage proposals, weddings, or even simple things such as dinner with an old friend. To this date, this channel is one of our most popular and has the most engagement. It helps our team members create windows to let others see into their personal lives and connect as a result.

▸ **Share learnings from feedback.** In chapter 4, we discussed the value of sharing and accepting feedback. I always encourage leaders to take this a step further by sharing changes they've made as a result of feedback or in response to mistakes. Having leaders step up and say, "I screwed up, and here's what I did about it," normalizes not only mistakes but also vulnerability. We have even started some of our quarterly extended leadership team meetings with everyone sharing something they did poorly over the last quarter and for which they would like a do-over. Our executive team always goes first.

Vulnerability doesn't develop in an organization overnight. But small steps like these can bring it about faster than you'd ever expect.

Better Communication

Having tackled sharing, it's crucial to focus on the other side of the equation. All the vulnerability in the world is useless unless the audience of that vulnerability responds with acceptance and understanding. Effective teams need to know how to turn sharing into actionable insights and how to communicate those insights in a way that strengthens relationships between managers and direct reports and between colleagues.

Poor communication can be a massive problem in an organization. A survey in the *Economist* found that 52 percent of respondents said communication breakdowns cause stress, and 44 percent said communication breakdowns were the number one cause of project failures. Perhaps most notably, a whopping 88 percent of millennial respondents believe that poor communication stunts career growth.[ii] In other words, most younger employees believe an organization that doesn't communicate well is capping their career potential—a damning belief for employees to hold.

A big part of improving communication comes from a mindset shift. A person cannot work well with others if they expect everyone else to think and feel the exact same way about things as they do. We all need to recognize that everyone is different and that there is rarely an objectively correct way to do or say something.

To illustrate this in practice, imagine that we have a manager, Taylor, and a direct report, Alex. Taylor is unapologetically candid and blunt. If a member of their team makes a mistake, Taylor usually doesn't sugarcoat the feedback and cuts straight to the point. What some may see as curt, Taylor sees as efficient—they prefer to receive feedback in this manner as well.

In contrast, Alex is, by their own admission, a bit sensitive and more introverted. Even though they've worked on accepting feedback and not taking criticism personally, Alex still feels a sharp, brief sting whenever their work is criticized.

As you can imagine, Taylor and Alex have a sharp personality difference that can cause problems. But the solution to this is not for either Taylor or Alex to completely change. Taylor cannot authentically become incredibly tactful and light-handed in delivering feedback overnight, and Alex won't easily suppress their feelings when hearing feedback. The solution is not to transfer Alex to a new team to avoid this friction either.

Instead, a leader should encourage Taylor and Alex to have an open conversation about their differences and see how they can meet each other halfway. Taylor can accommodate Alex in feedback conversations by being more mindful to slow down and consciously use a softer touch with their delivery. Conversely, Alex can work to not take what Taylor says personally and to appreciate that they are getting feedback directly rather than through the rumor mill. Taylor needs to know that dialing back their approach a notch actually ensures their message is better received, and Alex should understand that limiting raw emotion in response to feedback makes them appear more willing to learn.

As the manager, it falls on Taylor to initiate this type of communication shift. Here is how Taylor might go about having this type of open conversation:

"Alex, I would like to talk with you about our communication styles and how I deliver feedback. I know that, as a communicator, I tend to be very direct, and I admit that sometimes my feedback may come across as harsh or overcritical. I also realize that's not a perfect fit for how you prefer to get feedback, so I want to figure out how to build a bridge between my style and yours.

"First, I want to be clear that when I deliver feedback, the focus is always on your actions and where you can improve. I try very hard to never give feedback that feels like a personal attack or disrespectful of you. If I deliver feedback bluntly to you, it's not a judgment of you as a person, and it's not because I am upset with you or even because I think you are not performing well. It's simply that I prefer to give clear, in-the-moment feedback to help the people I manage understand precisely what I am looking for and grow from that experience.

"That being said, as your manager, I am committing to deliver

feedback in a way that is as considerate of your feelings and experience as possible, especially if it is on a sensitive topic. I will take extra time to really consider how I best reach you without diluting the actual point I am trying to make.

"But I also want to be realistic that this change isn't going to happen overnight. So as I do this work to add more care and tact to my feedback delivery to you, I ask that you remember that my directness is how I create clarity. What I want most is to give you ways to improve in a way that is easy to understand and with specific examples.

"I would also appreciate you helping me in this. If my feedback is well received, please tell me. If my feedback style is still not working well for you in some way, I'd love to know when that happens, and how you think I might be able to get the same point across in a way that you can receive more effectively. I know we can meet in the middle here and find a way to have these conversations in a manner that ensures the main message is communicated and that you feel valued and supported. Most importantly, this will leave us both feeling good about the interaction.

"How does this plan sound to you?"

Note how this example finds a happy medium between refusing to change and walking on eggshells. Building emotional capacity doesn't require teammates to change who they are or insulate themselves from people different from them.

Instead, what's key for managers and employees is to differentiate between what organizational psychologist and author Adam Grant calls task conflict and relationship conflict.[iii]

Task conflict occurs when a group of people disagree over ideas or opinions—everyone is united against one problem, even if they disagree on the solution. In contrast, relationship conflict occurs when these types of disagreements are filled with personal animosity, flared tempers, and even insults. While the latter type of conflict can tear teams apart, the former is an essential part of effective teams and partnerships. In the scenario above, Taylor is attempting to clearly differentiate between relationship and task feedback.

Strong emotional capacity allows teams to engage in task conflict without veering into relationship conflict. It involves getting differences out in the open, discussing ways to navigate those differences, and working together to bridge the divide. In other words, it's about progress, not perfection.

Pushing Limits

It's true that things like vulnerability and sharing are inherently uncomfortable for many people. What's crucial to know is that this is a feature, not a bug, of building emotional capacity.

As I wrote in *Elevate*, getting outside your comfort zone is absolutely critical to growth. Unfortunately, pushing a team to embrace uncomfortable situations can be challenging. We're in an era where it is more common to be shielded from uncomfortable or challenging situations. Too often, something that is beyond a person's comfort zone seems like a risk to avoid, not an opportunity for growth to embrace.

When members of a team are afraid to get outside their comfort zones, the result will be a status quo–oriented culture. As the saying goes, "If you do what you've always done, you'll get what you've always gotten."

That's why status quo–oriented companies don't lead their industries and eventually struggle to survive. Employees won't bring innovations to the table or be willing to pursue big ideas that may not work out—they'll just do things as they've always been done.

Leaders should encourage a culture where employees get out of their comfort zones in both top-down and individually driven ways. Here are a few more ideas to build safe discomfort into company meetings and team-building experiences:

► Consciously mix up groups at company events to ensure that employees can't always gravitate toward the people they know well. Companies can do this by randomizing lunch seating, creating cross-functional brainstorming or breakout groups, and other methods. For companies who are virtual or hybrid, this can also be done through company "speed-dating" events, where employees have to meet large numbers of team members in short bursts. It's particularly important to encourage intermingling between teams and departments—you'd be surprised the insights that can come when an accountant sits down with a salesperson or when an intern brings a fresh perspective in a conversation with an executive.

▶ Beyond that, don't make these mixed-group discussions surface level or solely work-related. Instead, encourage these inter-team or cross-department groups to share personal stories with each other. Even asking a breakout group at a company event to share one of their happiest moments from the past thirty days and one of their most challenging moments from the same period can really encourage people to push through the discomfort of sharing vulnerably and see that they can do so and be accepted.

▶ Bring world-class speakers who present different ways of thinking and demonstrate vulnerability to company events. I've found the most impactful speakers for our employees have been ones who detail real personal struggles as part of their narrative or presentation. At past company events, we've had speakers talk about surviving poverty and abuse as children, working to rehabilitate incarcerated felons, suffering extraordinary loss in a military battle, and more. These speakers don't just give our team perspective and make their challenges feel more conquerable—they also set the tone for greater vulnerability.

We try to encourage our teammates to push themselves out of their comfort zones outside the workday as well. I often talk about things I've done that scared me a little bit, such as signing up to bicycle from London to Paris in twenty-four hours as part of an event we planned for members of our team in the United Kingdom or signing up for an Olympic triathlon to force myself to train for something I had not done before.

I don't share these stories to highlight my own experiences or urge people to do these exact things. Instead, I share them to encourage team members to take similar risks and discover untapped potential within themselves.

This is also reinforced organically through the "What Made Your Week" channel referenced earlier—employees are always sharing new experiences they've tried, trips they've taken, or physical milestones they've hit. Creating a space for these experiences to be publicized fosters an environment where employees want to push themselves.

Like all other elements, emotional capacity is holistic. If a person pushes themselves out of their comfort zone in their personal life by traveling to a country they don't know, signing up for a race they haven't begun training for yet, or taking up a difficult new hobby, they will have more confidence outside their comfort zone at work as well, which will lead to more vulnerability, connection, and growth.

Ownership, Agency, and Control

Many teams and organizations are quick to take credit for things that go right but then blame any failures on factors beyond their control.

And there is no surer sign of an organization or leader with low emotional capacity than tolerating or embracing conspiracy theories as way of abdicating responsibly for poor outcomes.

Here's a perfect example.

During a conference a few years ago, an employee from a vendor in our industry, whom we had not been particularly close with over the years, approached one of our team members at an industry conference and declared that they knew, "for a fact," that our company accepted kickbacks, secretive payments from another competitive vendor who had become one of our biggest strategic partners. This "fact" had apparently circulated throughout the accuser's organization and was a regular talking point in the organization.

Needless to say, this "fact" was patently false. We've never accepted kickbacks from any of our partners, and we have gone on the record in saying that kickbacks should be eliminated entirely from our industry.

Why would a company spread such a rumor? It was pretty obvious: this company was frustrated that we were doing more business with this competitor of theirs than we were with them.

The reason was not nefarious or as a result of kickbacks. Instead, it was that the other vendor had developed into a better partner; their product was improving much faster with capabilities that many of our clients were asking for, their pricing was more favorable, and they had a clear agency partnership strategy, having built a four-person team dedicated to working with agencies such as ours.

Many of these considerations were sentiments we had shared with the jilted vendor on prior occasions, but rather than addressing the underlying issues, someone decided to invent and spread a conspiracy theory instead. This conspiracy theory became popular at the company because it let them off the hook by placing the failure outside their control rather than as a direct result of their product or service offering. The company was simply unable or unwilling to take ownership of these realities.

This is just one example of a phenomenon that's present in many facets of business. In a similar vein, I was once forwarded an email that was sent to one of our clients by a different partner in response to learning that the client had chosen a competitor's product over their own. The note to the client took a frustrated tone, spoke poorly of the competitor's product, and even made outright false assertions that bordered on slander. This response emanated from a culture within that sales team and organization that we had seen previously. Rather than looking inward after a poor outcome, they always assumed someone was out to get them.

This salesperson achieved two negative outcomes in this one message. First, they ruined any chance at working with that client in the future. Second, they didn't even ask for feedback or attempt to understand why the client made the decision they did. Getting that information might have helped them enhance a future pitch against the same competitor rather than create a detractor in the marketplace.

These examples—a conspiratorial approach to failure and a scorched-earth one—are hallmarks of low emotional capacity organizations.

Companies that always blame their failures on external circumstances struggle to improve because they never see anything as something they did wrong or where they could have done better. Conspiratorial thinking doesn't just distort the truth; it also prevents people and organizations from address and fixing their areas of weakness.

We saw the downside of a different version of this externally obsessed approach—and the upside of the opposite mindset—early in the pandemic. In March 2020, virtually every restaurant saw their traditional business grind to a halt, but two different courses of action were available at that inflection point. Some restaurants chose to simply surrender to their circumstances, choosing to hunker down and wait out the lockdowns until things returned to normal rather than make any major changes to their model. Many of these restaurants ended up shuttering permanently.

On the flip side, other restaurants accepted the reality of the situation and responded by setting up multiple delivery services, reorienting around takeout, constructing outdoor dining areas, and selling meal kits or wholesale bundles to meet existing demand. This group fared much better overall.

These two different strategies demonstrate a core element of emotional capacity. Organizations with low emotional capacity are regularly flattened by failure and adversity because they focus on what they don't or can't control. Organizations with high emotional capacity focus on what they do control and respond to adversity with resilience, accountability, and innovation.

Imagine two people get into a fender bender on their way to work. One person shakes it off, is grateful things weren't worse, and goes about their day as normal, while the other is furious all day, gets in a fight with their boss at the office, and shouts at their family when they arrive home. The key difference here isn't in the fender bender. Instead, the rest of the day is formed by each person's reaction to the same initiating event rather than the event itself—something that is fully within their control. In life and business, you can't always control what happens, but you can always control your reaction.

To build emotional capacity in their organizations, leaders must encourage their employees to take ownership over outcomes—both good and bad—and determine what is within their control and what is beyond it. Differentiating between problems we can solve through ownership and action and challenges we cannot influence and merely must withstand is crucial to building resilience and accountability.

For example, let's return to the example of a sales team that's lost a major sales pitch and is gearing up for another one in a few days.

A sales team with high emotional capacity would have someone from the sales team call the client and ask for their honest feedback, then share those notes openly with the sales team. They would also make a calculus similar to the one below, taking stock of what they can and cannot control going forward.

- **Can't control:** The outcome of the previous pitch. It's lost, so there's no reason to dwell on it beyond seeing what lessons can be learned.
- **Can control:** The content of their pitch deck and selling points. They can use the previous failure as both learning and motivation to assess their pitch and see if anything can be improved, which would be enhanced by any customer feedback.
- **Can't control:** How competitors will pitch or what their pricing and service level will be.
- **Can control:** Their level of knowledge about the prospect's needs and budget. This is especially true when pitching a public company—there is a ton of publicly available data that can be useful for a sales pitch. By learning more about the prospect, the sales team can adjust their pitch to better suit their needs.

There are always many factors that can sink a sales pitch that are outside the sales team's control. The prospect simply may not be in the right headspace to engage, or a desperate competitor may offer a far better price, to name a couple of examples.

But the sales team's level of preparation, their research, the questions they ask to understand the client, and their efforts to build a relationship are well within their control, and that's where they should focus.

Here are a few organizational best practices that encourage teams to learn from failure and avoid making the same mistakes twice:

▶ **Create an issue log.** This is an innovation from Ray Dalio, founder of Bridgewater Associates. Dalio and his team require employees to add any mistakes and failures they make to an issue log, which preserves those errors for future learning. In addition to getting your team more comfortable with mistakes and feedback, this is a great way to ensure your team learns from mistakes rather than dismisses them as due to outside circumstances.

▶ **Require debrief reports.** As discussed in the intellectual capacity chapter, we have made it a policy that managers complete a debrief form when we lose a client or make a major mistake, and then share that report with the team.

▶ **Ask for feedback.** When we've lost deals in the past, we've gained great insights by asking potential prospects why they chose a competitor, and we listen intently without judgment. There is rarely ever harm in asking for feedback, whether it's from a lost client or customer, a departing employee, an ending partnership, or otherwise. Getting this feedback is the best way to determine if the failure was due to something in your control that can be improved going forward or something outside your control that isn't worth losing sleep over. Here are several specific questions our sales team asks prospects whenever a pitch doesn't go their way:

- ► How did you hear about AP?
- ► What were you looking for in an affiliate marketing agency?
- ► What were your impressions of AP's solution?
- ► What AP resources/content were helpful to you?
- ► What other agencies did you include in your evaluation, and whom did you ultimately select? Why?
- ► What was your experience with AP like?
- ► Was AP not selected due to the presentation of solutions or the solution itself?
- ► Is there anything AP could have done differently?

Leaders with high emotional capacity don't fall back on excuses or present themselves as being at the mercy of external factors. Instead, these leaders and their teams take ownership of failure, learn from mistakes, grow stronger under adversity, and innovate their way to better outcomes with an eye toward what can be improved in the future.

Worry Not

When we asked a group of our leaders for their feedback about their experience at one of our leadership trainings months after the fact, the single most valuable lesson a group of our leaders took away surprisingly was not a core value discovery or a management tactic. Instead, it was a simple framework for a mindset shift.

The insight came from Warren Rustand, a decorated entrepreneur and educator who served as chairman or CEO of seventeen companies, as a board member for dozens more, and even worked in the White House with President Gerald Ford. In his speech on leadership, he shared a simple approach to energy management for leaders to think about in their personal and professional lives. He said, "If you don't control it, why worry about it? Because you don't control it. And if you do control it, why worry about it? Because you control it."

Rustand's emotional capacity is as high as any leader I've met. He's faced astonishing challenges in both his life and business career with the same even-keeled approach, examples of which he shared with the team.

Every business leader faces things beyond their control. The best managers lose people, the best salespeople lose deals, and the best companies lose market share due to changes in the market, such as recession or a new competitor. Emotional capacity is not about preventing these things from happening. Instead, it is about leaders training their teams to respond to these situations with poise and resilience.

Vulnerability and surrender of what we cannot control are not weaknesses; they're strengths that allow us to build better team bonds and dedicate our attention to what we *can* control. All other things—spiritual, intellectual, physical capacity—being equal, this last element is what separates the best teams, leaders, and organizations from the rest.

ACTION STEPS

Encouraging Vulnerability

▸ Read *One Last Talk* by Philip McKernan for a great explanation of the One Last Talk program described in this chapter. Also, check out my interview with Philip on the Elevate Podcast, linked at **robertglazer .com/eyt-resources**.

▸ Learn more about the Johari window and how to use it with your team, linked at **robertglazer .com/eyt-resources**.

▸ Start asking direct reports to share something from their personal lives that they're excited about in your check-ins and team meetings. If you aren't sure where to start, here are some good sample questions:

» What's a piece of good news in the past week/month from your personal and professional life?

» What's something you did in the past month that made you happy?

» What was your personal and professional best from the past week?

» What's a personal challenge you faced recently, and how did you respond to it?

» Advanced: What are the best and worst personal experiences you've had in the past week?

Embracing Productive Conflict

▸ Read *Think Again* by Adam Grant for a great distillation of task conflict versus relationship conflict and how great teams challenge each other without breaking trust or relationships.

Deepening Team Bonds

▸ At your next company, department, or team event, make a concerted effort to have your employees mix with people. Some ideas:

» Mix up seating throughout an event or meeting. At the beginning of a new session or day, ask everyone to sit next to someone they haven't spoken to at the event.

» Do a "Speed Dating" exercise where you have employees rotate through two-to-five minute conversations with partners, with a series of icebreaker questions to answer. This will allow each person to talk to several people and get to know them in a small amount of time.

» For a lunch, dinner, or breakout group exercises, set up a seating chart that ensures each table/group has members of multiple teams and departments to ensure inter-team mingling.

» Consider doing a "connection contest" at company events. A great way to do this is to create a passport book with a page with each person's information, a question you need to get answered about them, and a place for them to sign. You can then give prizes to the people who make the most one-on-one connections.

Chapter Six

CAPACITY BUILDING AND PEOPLE MANAGEMENT

"There is no way to spend too much time on obtaining and developing the best people."

—Larry Bossidy

We've discussed all four capacities and shared detailed strategies for building each one throughout an entire organization. The one thing we haven't discussed, which is equally as important, is how capacity aligns with an organization's talent acquisition, evaluation, and development strategy.

There are three key concepts to understand as you lead your organization down the capacity building path:

1. How capacity building affects who you bring into your organization.

2. How capacity building impacts who you elevate into higher roles in your organization.

3. How to use capacity building to make sure you have the right career paths at your organization.

As with most things in your organization, everything else gets easier if you start by hiring the right people.

Building an A-Team

Imagine you're interviewing two candidates for a sales role. Each candidate generated $1 million in sales in the past year. However, one candidate took seven years to reach that $1 million level, while the other hit that benchmark in just the second year of their sales career. All other things being equal, who do you choose?

Many companies would hire the candidate with more "experience," especially for the same salary. But if you're hiring based on a person's future performance rather than past accomplishments, the calculus changes.

Wouldn't you rather have the person who rapidly improved and reached the same milestone faster? Don't you think the person who demonstrated an ability to build capacity faster will likely reach the $2 million sales level faster than the more experienced candidate?

On top of that, when you hire someone with more experience than you need, they often come into the role overqualified and overpaid, which is never a great place to start. People who are overqualified tend to feel they are above the responsibilities of their role. Plus, in many cases, these candidates come from larger companies where they haven't had to get their hands dirty for some time; they are used to having a bigger team that does the actual work. So rather than roll up their sleeves and do work that is beneath them, they often start by hiring other people.

A candidate with significant experience often enters your organization with the level of skill or experience needed at that moment in time. The problem occurs when you soon realize that while they have the skills you need today, they may lack the ability to keep up with the company's trajectory and be the leader you'll need tomorrow. If your experienced hire can't build their capacity quickly, they may be in over their head before you know it.

This may be part of the reason why so many hires don't work out. The executive search firm Heidrick & Struggles found that 40 percent of senior executives hired in America either quit or are transitioned out of an organization within eighteen months.[i] And many companies have similar rates of hiring failure throughout their organization.

This problem is exacerbated in a high-growth company. Fast-growing organizations, in all industries, need to constantly add higher-level roles in each of the organization's functions. They may hire someone at a manager level in marketing to lead the marketing team, but it won't be long before they need a director or an executive-level leader in that same department. It can be hard to find the right person for your team today when you may need an entirely different level of work from that person within a couple of years or even a few months.

The key to getting sustained growth without churning through employees or gambling on external leadership hires is to identify people who show the ability to build their capacity quickly, get them into your organization, and invest in their development. Even if these high-aptitude candidates or employees are a bit below the experience line when they join or are promoted, their improvement trajectory will push them up to or above the growth rate faster than you'd think.

You may recall the capacity building chart shared in the first chapter of this book. This iteration of that same capacity building chart clarifies the distinction between high-experience hires and high-capacity hires who demonstrate greater potential capacity. The terms *high capacity* and *high aptitude* are interchangeable.

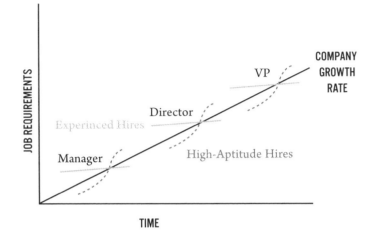

Using the graph above as an illustration, you can see that it's better to hire or promote people who follow the dashed lines' trajectory, rather than the solid lines' path. People with faster career momentum will eventually outperform lower-capacity people with more experience.

To put this in concrete terms, you should evaluate potential hires based on whether they are likely to be accountable for the outcomes you need them to achieve in the future, not based on what they've accomplished in the past. Experience is certainly part of that equation but is often overvalued if it took a long time to attain. Initially, high-capacity, low-experience people will be in over their heads when they step into a new role. But this is a case where you're accepting some short-term growing pains to get a long-term win. When people with a track record of growth take on a role that's a bit beyond their experience level or qualifications, they feel compelled to give it their all, learn as much as they can, and prove they were worthy of the trust that was placed in them.

With high-capacity people, you are investing in a growth stock—a riskier bet with a higher upside. With high-experience people, you are investing in a bond—a safe bet that has less upside. Fast-growing companies need more of the former and fewer of the latter. Experience is great, but in a growth company, experience will expire and become irrelevant faster than you think.

From a hiring standpoint, particularly for important roles and functions, this is the key to bringing in people who won't be overtaken by a company's growth curve. Ideally, you want employees who have enough experience to do the job but also have the capacity for growth. If you can't have both, you'll probably want more of the latter.

Here are some ways to identify high-capacity candidates:

▸ **Promotion in place.** Many people only gain promotions and higher titles in their careers by switching jobs. While these people can be high-capacity employees too, you should gravitate toward people who have been promoted quickly and multiple times within a single organization where they stayed for a few years. There are two reasons for this. First, sometimes people job hop because they are unable to advance within their company—switching jobs can hide a lack of growth or talent. Second, if you think a candidate who has cycled through three companies in three years will stay at your organization for long, you are fooling yourself.

► **Renaissance people.** People who have proven themselves in a wide range of roles, projects, or skill sets tend to be fast learners who adapt to change and will step up to do whatever the organization needs at a given time. If you encounter a candidate who jumped from marketing to sales to client services within the same organization and excelled at all three, that candidate deserves a closer look.

► **Drive to learn.** This is an easy one to identify in an interview. You can almost always tell if someone is obsessed with learning when you talk to them. See how they respond when you ask them what books they've read, what they've done to learn and grow within their role, and what they've done to take ownership of their own group. If a candidate's eyes light up and they engage intently when you ask these types of questions, you're probably talking to a voracious learner.

► **Overperformance on goals.** When you interview candidates, ask for specific information on the expectations they faced and their performance relative to those benchmarks. If a candidate can outline how they have consistently exceeded expectations or metrics in their role, that's a good sign. Sales leaders are very good at asking these kinds of questions for salespeople and can probably help you.

▸ **Pull, not push.** If a candidate has changed jobs often, it's actually a good sign if that is a result of former managers or colleagues recruiting them to join a new organization. Low-capacity people get a new job by selling themselves to people who haven't worked with them before; high-capacity people are recruited by people they've worked with because they've proven themselves to be top performers. I am always a bit wary of someone who has gotten deep into their career and gotten every new role through a job listing or a recruiter they did not know previously rather than from someone within their existing professional network. That means the people who know them the best are the least interested in hiring them again. Red flag!

▸ **Personal grit.** High-capacity people often demonstrate their growth potential in their personal lives as well. It's helpful to get a sense of whether a candidate has a personal passion that they've stuck with and improved at over the past few years. Some of the highest capacity people I've met are former competitive athletes, dedicated musicians, passionate artists, or devoted writers who have constantly worked hard to improve their craft.

While not every high-capacity person demonstrates these qualities, someone who has all or most of these boxes checked is likely to be a fast riser. If you screen for these qualities, the result will be a steady supply of talent that is ready to grow with your organization.

Capacity Building Still Requires Hard Choices

Of course, capacity building has its limits. The fastest-growing companies sometimes exceed the growth rate of all but their very best performers. This in turn puts leaders in an awkward position: they need to evaluate whether giving an employee a step up on the ladder is a feasible challenge or whether elevating that person will have negative consequences for both the employee and the company.

For example, a friend of mine knew he needed a CFO for his hyper-growth company, which was growing more than 100 percent each year. His smart, loyal controller badly wanted the job; she had grown used to being the leader of the finance team and was insulted at the idea of having someone hired above her. Though my friend thought the employee wasn't ready, he promoted her anyway because he was afraid of losing her.

Shortly after taking the CFO seat, the employee made a mistake that cost the company $1 million; the error was a direct result of not having the experience or capacity at that point in time to take on CFO-level responsibilities.

Though she made the error, the real failure was at the leadership level: my friend knew the company needed an experienced CFO, did not believe the employee could deliver what was needed at that level, and should never have promoted her into that position. He was afraid to upset her by hiring above her, so he made the more comfortable choice in the moment—and ended up creating much more discomfort later.

Capacity building is dependent on accountability. When you build your own capacity, you must be accountable to your vision for your personal growth. When you build your team's capacity, you need to balance your belief in your people with a clear-eyed understanding of where any given employee's capacity is relative to the needs and deliverables of the role.

It's a delicate balancing act to be an encouraging advocate and a pragmatic evaluator simultaneously, but that is what the best leaders and coaches do. They coach their players to play to their highest level and know when they need to come out of the game.

One of the worst things a leader can do is let someone continue to flounder in a role in which they are not performing well or let someone who hasn't improved enough advance due to loyalty, nostalgia, or fear of rocking the boat. As my friend learned, simply promoting someone when they're not ready or don't have the right skills and hoping for the best can have dire consequences for both the employee and the company.

The reality is that in many cases, it's necessary to bring in more qualified or experienced people to serve in critical leadership roles, often at the director and VP level. Many employees who have been with an organization for several years struggle with these types of personnel moves, especially if they were the top person in that function with a lower-level title. For example, if a director of finance is used to being the highest-ranking finance employee at an organization, they may bristle at the idea of having a VP of finance or CFO hired above them.

Change can be hard, and pride is a powerful force; it often clouds people's self-awareness in objectively evaluating their own abilities relative to the organization's needs. That director of finance might have still been improving at a strong rate and could have even been recently promoted. They just weren't quite ready for that next step, but the company needed someone in that role sooner rather than later.

A surprising percentage of people in this scenario won't be able to make this psychological adjustment and will end up leaving your organization. In all likelihood, these people would be better off learning from someone who is better qualified for the role and who can even mentor them. Time and time again as we built AP, I saw pride get in the way of what was clearly the right choice for both the organization and the individual; the only good solution was to amicably decide to part ways with the employee and wish them the best. Often, it's only with some distance years later that these employees will admit to you that they were in over their head, and you made the right choice.

While capacity building will put leaders in the best possible position to elevate top performers as the company grows, it's important to recognize that every person has limits, and those limits need to balance with what the organization objectively needs at any given moment in time.

Building Better Career Paths

Capacity building in an organization can also create better alignment between individual and organizational wants and needs. The most effective teams are built on placing the right person in the right role at the right time. We saw in the spiritual capacity chapter how organizations can identify people's strengths and use that knowledge to match employees to roles where they'll thrive and want to stay long term.

At many organizations, there is an established norm that the only way for employees to advance is to become a manager or even to lead an entire team. This path doesn't suit everyone, however. While a key responsibility of a leader is to identify and develop new leaders, it's also important to make sure the people identified for leadership roles actually want to lead.

Leadership is a unique skill. Many strong individual contributors who are excellent at what they do don't have the skill set or desire to be a leader. Leadership is about the success of your team, and many individual contributors are primarily motivated by their own contributions.

Putting strong individual contributors who don't want to manage into manager roles is a no-win scenario—the individual contributor gets stuck with a manager role they don't enjoy, their direct reports aren't managed well, and the company loses the individual contributor's output *and* adds a subpar manager to their ranks. And few things can hurt a company's retention rates more than bad management. For example, a Gallup survey found that 75 percent of employees who exit a job list their manager as the number one motivation for their departure.[ii]

The onus is on you as a leader to help your employees find the right path for them, a process that is made much easier when they understand more about themselves and how their strengths and career goals align with the expectations and desired outcomes of a role.

Here's how you can help build a better path for individual contributors in your organization:

- **Create "senior" individual contributor roles.** While the head of a department usually manages a team, many departments also need exceptional individual contributors who want to improve at their craft. An exceptional accountant, salesperson, product manager, engineer, or demand generation specialist should be able to advance in their discipline and earn raises without having to take on managing a team.

- **Focus on outcomes.** An individual contributor's daily workload and responsibilities look very different from a manager's. Often, individual contributors have fewer meetings and more opportunities for deep, focused work. As a result, individual contributors should be held accountable for clear outcomes that are tied to the company's bottom line—or at least to their department's most important metrics.

- **Compensate individual contributors fairly.** The reason many people who don't want to manage end up as managers is simple economics—the highest rungs of the organizational ladder are occupied by managers, and those levels are where the money often is. This is why organizations should align pay for individual contributors to the output they deliver for the organization. A brilliant engineer, a top salesperson, a recruiter who constantly brings in top talent, or a client retention specialist who rarely loses a client might actually create more value for an organization than a manager. For individual contributors, determine what their contribution is worth to the organization and pay them accordingly, no managerial duties required.

These steps create a viable path for individual contributors to continue to build capacity. It's also a good idea to give new managers a rip cord they can pull if and when they realize that management was not the right choice, which happens regularly. It's important for leaders to set the expectation with new managers that it's okay to decide management is not for them and redirect them to the individual contributor path.

Right People, Right Seats

The most valuable outcome of capacity building in an organization is to ensure the right people are in the right roles as the company scales. Use this chapter as a road map for putting capacity building into practice in your talent development strategy. Start by hiring talent that demonstrates the ability to build capacity. Train them and continue to build their capacity holistically. Ensure they are put on the right path that maximizes their strengths—even if it isn't management. And finally, be aware that doing all of this well won't solve all your problems. There will still be hard choices where you'll need to hire above someone or take them out of a role that's become over their head.

Capacity building is a tool for making your people consistently better as well as a rubric for aligning your employees to the best roles. Job performance is not a fixed output—the same employee may be fantastic in one role or at one job level but overwhelmed or ineffective in another. Always remember that it's on leaders to ensure the right people are in the right role and empowered to do their best work.

ACTION STEPS

Hiring High-Capacity Employees

- For advice on hiring, I highly recommend *Who* by Dr. Geoff Smart. The book will teach you how to create a repeatable, scientific hiring process and help you ensure your team asks behavioral questions that identify the markers of high-capacity people in the interview process.

Making Hard Choices in Talent Management

▸ Read *Powerful* by former Netflix Chief Talent Officer Patty McCord, which offers one of the best guides to making hard talent development choices that I've ever encountered. Also, check out my interview with Patty on the Elevate Podcast, linked at **robertglazer.com/eyt-resources.**

▸ Check out my TEDx Talk on open transitions titled "It's Time To End Two Weeks Notice." Making hard talent development choices is easier when you have an open, humane way to handle employee departures, and this talk shares a method we've pioneered at AP. It is linked at **robertglazer.com /eyt-resources**.

Chapter Seven

BUILDING A PATH

"There is no success without succession."

—Business Proverb

Projected on the massive LED screen was a statistic I had seen many times. This time, it had a very different meaning.

It was December 2021, and we were doing a dress rehearsal for our annual AP Summit, which was being held virtually due to the pandemic and filmed in a professional studio. The graphic on the screen showed one of our core company objectives: "The vast majority of our senior leaders have been promoted from within." As the graphic flashed across the screen, the speaker noted for the audience that over 80 percent of the leaders in our company had been promoted internally.

What made the concept particularly resonant that morning

was not the thirty-foot screen displaying the message; it was that it was being delivered by my longtime number two, Matt Wool. We were about to announce to the company that I was handing the reins to Matt following a two-year, carefully orchestrated succession plan, and Matt was practicing his first speech as the new CEO of AP and sharing his vision for the future of the business.

After years of pushing the concept of capacity building in our organization—and seeing tremendous growth as a result—this decision to step aside brought our dedication to the principle to its logical endpoint.

Throughout this book, we have explored detailed methods for building your team's capacity. However, all that effort and investment will only be effective if an organization's leadership embraces the inevitable outcome of capacity building: succession.

To truly develop a growth culture where employees are constantly growing along with the business, leaders must recognize that they may be training people whose capacity growth trajectory will necessitate providing new and increasing responsibilities to keep them engaged in the long run. The fact is that leaders can either give their fastest-growing talent more responsibilities and opportunities at their organization, or they can watch as they get those same opportunities elsewhere. Accepting this reality and making hard choices to ensure other companies don't reap the rewards of your capacity-building investments is a crucial part of leadership and building an enduring organization.

Three Paths

Companies can take three fundamental approaches with the upwardly mobile talent in their organization. These approaches are Star Stifling, Catch and Release, and Pure Meritocracy.

A Star Stifler is usually a slower-growth organization where managers and leaders see rising talent as a threat to their jobs. These organizations don't invest in their star talent; in fact, incumbent managers often actively stunt their people's growth by withholding high-leverage projects, not offering development opportunities, or not highlighting their performance to senior leadership. Because these organizations don't grow fast, advancement opportunities are even more rare—a promotion often requires pushing someone off the rung above them on the ladder rather than constantly offering new ladders to climb.

Star Stiflers experience a consistent drain of talent over time. Their best people inevitably realize there are other organizations where they will be valued more, and they will take the first opportunity possible to jump to those workplaces. The employees who stay long term are often mediocre performers who have mastered the company's political game. The result is that the people in leadership have far more internal value than objective external value, and they hold information close to consolidate their power. At the end of the day, their real value is that they know the company and its politics inside and out, know the right people to please, and therefore can often get by doing the bare minimum.

Star Stiflers value tenure over talent and politics over potential. I experienced this approach at the first company I worked at in my career, a strategy consulting firm named Arthur D. Little. ADL had some phenomenal junior talent during my tenure, all of whom left the organization within a few years and went on to prominent leadership roles and incredible careers elsewhere. These strong performers were often blocked by an entrenched group of low-quality leaders who had mastered the company politics and led the firm to bankruptcy in 2002.[i]

Needless to say, Star Stiflers are not committed to capacity building; these companies are often where talent goes to die, and mediocrity just tries to hang on long enough to retire.

The second approach is Catch and Release. A Catch and Release organization invests in its people and takes pride in their growth inside the company. However, eventually these organizations also recognize that their rising stars may have more opportunities outside the company. In turn, leaders in Catch and Release organizations actively help their best people find roles outside the company once they realize these employees are either being held back or are ready for an opportunity their organization cannot offer anytime soon.

A great example of the Catch and Release approach is the culture former Netflix Chief Talent Officer Patty McCord helped build at the streaming giant. McCord and her team recognized that they would see several of their top performers eventually run out of room to advance. Knowing this, they created an innovative and humane way of handling employee departures, encouraging open employee transitions and a culture where it was a source of pride for people to go elsewhere and to "be from Netflix."[ii]

A Catch and Release company can also often lose senior talent when there are multiple people vying for a single leadership role. There is often the understanding that if a candidate for a senior role is not selected, they will want to pursue that same level of role at another organization and will find substantial demand for their services. This was the case when legendary General Electric CEO Jack Welch selected his successor in 2001 from three internal candidates; it was widely expected in the moment that the other finalists for the job would be offered CEO roles at other companies, and that is exactly what happened.[iii]

It is certainly noble that Catch and Releasers are willing to lose their best people in order to help those stars reach new heights. However, this policy might not always lead to positive outcomes, especially when a company known for developing talent has their competitors frequently poach their employees by offering promotions, elevated responsibilities, and/or compensation beyond their current level. In these cases, an organization might become a competitor's training ground.

Sometimes, the Catch and Releaser makes the correct calculation when they let someone leave—the employee truly isn't ready to elevate, and their subsequent performance with the new organization proves that hypothesis correct. This happens frequently in professional sports when a player from one team is offered substantially more money and/or a bigger role to join a new team. The star's current team may decide that, while the player is talented, their performance is bolstered by a great culture, excellent teammates, or a coaching strategy that emphasizes their strengths and hides their weaknesses. Remember, similar to the current employer, the existing team sees this player every day in practice, so they should have the most comprehensive perspective when establishing the player's value to the organization. In a large percentage of these cases, the player who is signed away for big money underperforms their contract with their new team. The data backs this up; only 50 percent of National Football League free agent contracts, which are not guaranteed, end up lasting even two years.[iv]

But in some cases, Catch and Release organizations watch a former employee go on to be a transformational leader for another company, or even a competitor, because they were too slow to recognize the person's potential and clear the path in front of them for the right opportunity. No matter how effective a Catch and Releaser is at evaluating their own talent, these situations will happen, and they are usually painful.

The last type of approach, and probably the rarest, is a Pure Meritocracy. Pure Meritocracies make the same talent development investment as Catch and Releasers. The crucial difference is that when they realize that a rising star is a better fit for the organization than someone currently in a role, they are unafraid to make that switch.

If you will allow me one last sports analogy, I think it will demonstrate one of the best instances of an organization that consistently embraces the Pure Meritocracy approach and how it changed the course of history. Bill Belichick, the head coach of the New England Patriots NFL football team, is considered one of the greatest coaches in the history of sports, and his biggest advantage may be his total objectivity when evaluating talent. Belichick only retains and gives playing time to the players who contribute most to the Patriots' chances of winning as a team today. He is not influenced by a player's reputation, contract, potential, seniority, or history of past performance.

In 2001, Belichick's starting quarterback, Drew Bledsoe, suffered a brutal injury in the second game of the season. Bledsoe was a former number one pick in the NFL Draft, was the face of the New England Patriots franchise, had just signed a $103 million contract, and had previously played in a Super Bowl.[v] But Belichick soon realized that his team was performing better with Bledsoe's backup starting at quarterback, even though that backup nearly went undrafted and hadn't started an NFL game before that season. When Bledsoe was finally healthy enough to play, Belichick made the unpopular decision to keep him on the bench in favor of his backup, who had just led the team to a near win against the St. Louis Rams, who had the best record in the league at the time.

If you don't know who the backup is by now, you'll certainly recognize his name: it was Tom Brady, who led the Patriots to the first of six Super Bowl championships that same season by beating those same St. Louis Rams. Brady is generally recognized as the greatest quarterback in NFL history, but that statement might not be true today had he been forced to the bench out of a sense of loyalty or nostalgia.

In a Pure Meritocracy, the most talented, qualified person in a given moment gets the job. Tenure is never viewed as an advantage or assumed to result in better performance.

Pure Meritocracies are likely to get the best results, but the reality is that it's hard for most organizations to follow this approach all the time. It does create some very uncomfortable moments, especially if leaders are fearful of losing their jobs to up-and-comers. At the same time, no leader wants to be responsible for the business equivalent of stifling Tom Brady on the bench or watching him beat you on another team; there will be times when outcomes take precedence over feelings.

Most of these moments involve determining what to do when a rising star's growth path becomes "blocked" by a more senior or tenured employee, especially one with less upside. Many companies with potential stars in these scenarios are hesitant to rock the boat, even when losing or suppressing extraordinary talent is rarely in the best interest of the business.

For years, our organization was a Catch and Releaser. Echoing McCord's words, I was proud to see people "be from AP" and go on to bigger and better roles. We've even reaped the added benefit of having some of our former employees turn into clients or strategic partners.

But we've also seen important opportunities to lean into the Pure Meritocracy approach, especially when failing to do so would mean losing a top performer with the potential to lead at the highest level of the organization.

This, after all, is the definition of an organization that fully embraces capacity building, which brings us back to the chart shared in the beginning of the book.

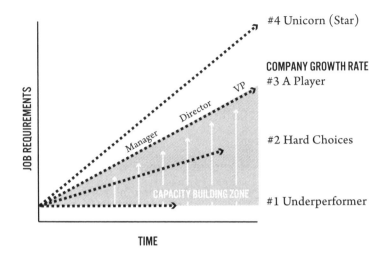

A large portion of this book has been focused on coaching people up to the top of the Capacity Building Zone. But the people who are already at or above the Company Growth require your attention as well. As you recruit and develop more A-Players and Unicorns, it's crucial to develop a clear path for their ascension within the organization. You never want to lose a Unicorn because someone in the lower region of the CBZ is blocking their path.

All of this brings me back to my own difficult decision to step aside as CEO.

Over the years, I've seen many leaders' identities become intertwined with their roles in a business; this is especially common with entrepreneurs, founders, or CEOs. The prestige and admiration so many leaders experience in their role cause them to lose sight of what they really want or what their business needs. The reality is that leaders should be regularly evaluating both their wants and the business's needs, which requires real reflection, a suppression of ego, and acknowledging what is objectively true.

Sometimes, a moment of truth comes because a leader's professional passions are no longer aligned with what the organization needs. A sales leader may realize that they don't want to manage a massive sales organization—they may simply want to sell and enjoy the high of chasing deals and closing business rather than having the pressure of leading, holding others accountable, or having difficult performance management conversations.

But in other cases, this decision point arrives when a leader realizes someone on their team is ready and better qualified to take the reins—and that giving them the reins is the best decision for everyone involved.

In a way, these two factors converged when I decided to promote Matt to CEO and step into a different role.

First, I came to realize over the past few years through thoughtful reflection that what I love most is building, creating, and teaching. The moments I enjoyed most as CEO were elevating people on my team, identifying a vision for the future of our industry, helping our emerging leaders build their capacity, and seeing team members reap the rewards of something they helped build. While these priorities might perfectly suit the CEO of a fifty-person company, these are not the primary responsibilities of a CEO of a global company approaching three hundred employees, which is what we were at the time.

The CEO of a larger company has three key duties: to set the organization's strategy, to be accountable for its results, and to build, lead, and manage the team of executive officers. While I could do these things, they were not the areas where I felt I could make my greatest contribution to our business or where I would be most fulfilled. Plus, it was clear that there was someone else at the organization who could fulfill these responsibilities more effectively: Matt.

Matt's story is arguably the ultimate example of capacity building at AP. Matt was our fourth employee, and he rose through the ranks of the organization from VP of Client Services to General Manager to President, where he led the company's day-to-day operations for over five years and built out our executive team.

Over many years, Matt continued to build his capacity and did the hard work to prepare himself to lead an organization. He developed the spiritual capacity to better understand himself and his authentic leadership style, the intellectual capacity to deeply understand every area of our business, the physical capacity to be resilient while leading our business through a global pandemic, and the emotional capacity to earn the respect of our clients, vendors, employees, and investors.

Matt was ready to be a CEO. I didn't want to risk losing him by letting my ego get in the way or refusing to make a difficult decision that I knew was right. This was a rare situation where we managed to achieve the best outcome for me, Matt, and the business at the same time.

While CEO successions are less frequent, similar situations arise at every rung of an organization regularly. Every leader in an organization needs to reflect periodically on whether their individual contributors should get opportunities to lead teams, whether their team leaders should get opportunities to lead departments, and whether department heads have a shot to ascend to the executive level.

These opportunities do not happen naturally. Leaders must be intentional in creating a talent development strategy dedicated to capacity building to be in the position to have a surplus of talent.

Every leader in an organization has two key decisions in the capacity building arena.

The first decision is whether to help their people get better at their current jobs or whether to help them get better overall. If you've made it this far, you'll likely recognize the latter is a better choice.

The second decision comes only after an organization has fully instilled capacity building into every level of the company. Then, the choice for leaders is to decide whether to be threatened by the stars who rise from within their teams, departments, or companies or to give those stars opportunities to advance and become the organizations' next leaders. The former approach may lead to a stronger sense of stability or security—holding on to a job by suppressing the competition—but the latter approach is the essence of true leadership and the way to build a great, enduring company.

What kind of team do you want to build? What type of organization do you want to lead? What type of leadership legacy do you want to leave? If you've built your own spiritual capacity, the answers to these questions will be much clearer.

For those who want to build enduring organizations or best-in-class teams, I believe deeply that this is the ultimate playbook. Capacity building is the system to build your business by building your people and ensuring the best possible outcomes for employees, leaders, and the organization as a whole.

ACKNOWLEDGMENTS

Writing a book requires a village and I am incredibly thankful for my village.

To the amazing team at Acceleration Partners (AP) and our next generation of leaders. I am inspired by watching each of you work to build your capacity and look forward to watching you continue to grow and ascend into our future leaders of tomorrow.

To my editing team of Mick Sloan and Tucker Max. Mick read countless drafts, provided important insights, tracked down research, and is primarily responsible for interpreting all my typos and missing words. Tucker, I so appreciate your candid, incisive, and often quite funny commentary in the margins. Honestly, I got used to the red ink and was worried when it started to disappear.

To Richard Pine, Alexis Hurley, and the entire Inkwell Management team for their ongoing support and partnership for all of my books.

To my editor, Meg Gibbons, for her continued support for my writing and new projects and for being such a champion of the capacity building concept. Also, to Dominique Raccah, Liz Kelsch, Morgan Vogt, Kavita Wright, Kay Birkner, and the entire Sourcebooks team for their hard work on the launch.

Last, but never least, this book is dedicated to my wife, Rachel, and to my three children.

It is because of Rachel's endless support that I am able to focus on my writing and my work, which often requires long hours and travel.

Chloe, Max and Zach, there is no role in life that I would want more than being your dad. I love watching each of you continue to grow and develop into the best version of yourself and know you will each make an impact on the world in your own unique way.

NOTES

Chapter Two: Build Your Team's Spiritual Capacity

i   "What Are the Four Domains of CliftonStrengths?," Gallup, accessed May 6, 2022, https://www.gallup.com/cliftonstrengths/en/253736/cliftonstrengths-domains.aspx.

ii Simon Sinek, *Start with Why: How Great Leaders Inspire Everyone to Take Action* (New York: Portfolio, 2009).

iii "Why Discovery," WHY Institute, accessed May 6, 2022, https://whyinstitute.com/why-discovery/.

Chapter Three: Build Your Team's Intellectual Capacity

i   Abigail Johnson Hess, "LinkedIn: 94% of Employees Say They Would Stay at a Company Longer for This Reason—And It's Not a Raise," CNBC, February 27, 2019, https://www.cnbc.com/2019/02/27/94percent-of-employees-would-stay-at-a-company-for-this-one-reason.html.

ii "Reading Improves Memory, Concentration and Stress," North central University, September 21, 2015, https://www.ncu.edu/blog/reading-improves-memory-concentration-and-stress.

iii David Epstein, *Range: Why Generalists Triumph In A Specialized World* (New York: Riverhead Books, 2019), 77.

iv   Hal Elrod, *The Miracle Morning: The Not-So-Obvious Secret Guaranteed to Transform Your Life Before 8AM* (Temecula, CA: Hal Elrod International, 2012).

Chapter Four: Build Your Team's Physical Capacity

i   Eugene Kim, "Yahoo CEO Marissa Mayer Worked from Her Hospital Bed Shortly After Having Twins," *Business Insider*, June 6, 2016, https://www.businessinsider.com/marissa-mayer-worked-in-hospital-after-having-twins-2016-6.

ii   A. M. Williamson and Anne-Marie Feyer, "Moderate Sleep Deprivation Produces Impairments in Cognitive and Motor Performance Equivalent to Legally Prescribed Levels of Alcohol Intoxication," *Occupational and Environmental Medicine* 57, no. 10 (October 2000): 649–55, http://dx.doi.org/10.1136/oem.57.10.649.

iii   Pavithra Mohan, "15 CEOs on How Much Sleep They Actually Get," *Fast Company*, August 2, 2019, https://www.fastcompany.com/90380247/15-ceos-on-how-much-sleep-they-actually-get.

iv   Dave Schools, "Exactly How Much Sleep Mark Zuckerberg, Jack Dorsey, and Other Successful Business Leaders Get," *Inc.*, March 6, 2017, https://www.inc.com/dave-schools/exactly-how-much-sleep-mark-zuckerberg-jack-dorsey-and-other-successful-business.html.

v   Eric Suni, "How Much Sleep Do We Really Need?," Sleep Foundation, April 13, 2022, https://www.sleepfoundation.org/how-sleep-works/how-much-sleep-do-we-really-need.

vi   Ray Maurer, "Remote Employees Are Working Longer Than Before," SHRM, December 16, 2020, https://www.shrm.org/hr-today/news/hr-news/pages/remote-employees-are-working-longer-than-before.aspx.

vii   "Long working hours increasing deaths from heart disease and stroke: WHO, ILO," World Health Organization, May 17, 2021, https://www.who.int/news/item/17-05-2021-long-working-hours-increasing-deaths-from-heart-disease-and-stroke-who-ilo.

viii "Workplace Burnout Survey," Deloitte, accessed on April 17, 2022, https://www2.deloitte.com/us/en/pages/about-deloitte/articles/burnout-survey.html.

ix "Exercise Can Boost Your Memory and Thinking Skills," Harvard Health Publishing, February 15, 2021, https://www.health.harvard.edu/mind-and-mood/exercise-can-boost-your-memory-and-thinking-skills.

x Matt Weinberger and Paige Leskin, "The Rise and Fall of Marissa Mayer, the Once-Beloved CEO of Yahoo Now Pursuing Her Own Venture," *Business Insider*, February 11, 2020, https://www.businessinsider.com/yahoo-marissa-mayer-rise-and-fall-2017-6; Eugene Kim, "Yahoo Insiders Are So Fed Up with Marissa Mayer That They've Apparently Come Up with a Snarky Nickname for Her," *Business Insider*, January 11, 2016, https://www.businessinsider.com/marissa-mayer-is-called-evita-2016-1.

xi Sophie Kleeman, "Here's What Happened to All 53 of Marissa Mayer's Yahoo Acquisitions," Gizmodo, June 15, 2016, https://gizmodo.com/heres-what-happened-to-all-of-marissa-mayers-yahoo-acqu-1781980352.

xii Alina Selyukh, "Every Yahoo Account That Existed in Mid-2013 Was Likely Hacked," NPR, October 3, 2017, https://www.npr.org/sections/thetwo-way/2017/10/03/555016024/every-yahoo-account-that-existed-in-mid-2013-was-likely-hacked.

Chapter Five: Build Your Team's Emotional Capacity

i "Johari Window: A Model for Self-Awareness, Personal Development, Group Development, and Understanding Relationship," University of Wisconsin, 2003, https://apps.cfli.wisc.edu/johari/support/JohariExplainChapman2003.pdf.

ii "Communication Barriers in the Modern Workplace," *Economist* Intelligence Unit, 2018, https://impact.economist.com/perspectives/sites/default/files/EIU_Lucidchart

-Communication%20barriers%20in%20the%20modern%
20workplace.pdf.

iii   Adam Grant, *Think Again: The Power of Knowing What You Don't Know* (New York: Viking, 2021), 78–80.

Chapter Six: Capacity Building and People Management

i   George Bradt, "Heidrick and Struggles Study of 20,000 Searches Highlights Need for Onboarding Improvements," Prime Genesis, April 2009, https://www.primegenesis.com/our-blog/2009/04/40-percent-of-execs-pushed-out-fail-or-quit-within-18-months.

ii   Jennifer Robison, "Turning Around Employee Turnover," Gallup, May 8, 2008, https://news.gallup.com/businessjournal/106912/turning-around-your-turnover-problem.aspx.

Chapter Seven: Building a Path

i   Jonathan D. Glater, "Arthur D. Little Plans Bankruptcy Filing," *New York Times*, February 6, 2002, https://www.nytimes.com/2002/02/06/business/arthur-d-little-plans-bankruptcy-filing.html.

ii   Vivian Giang, "She Created Netflix's Culture and It Ultimately Got Her Fired," *Fast Company*, February 17, 2016, https://www.fastcompany.com/3056662/she-created-netflixs-culture-and-it-ultimately-got-her-fired.

iii   Geoffrey Colvin, "Some People Think Jack Welch Is Irreplaceable. Not Welch. Here Is the Inside Story of How He and the GE Board Selected His Successor," *Fortune*, January 8, 2001, https://archive.fortune.com/magazines/fortune/fortune_archive/2001/01/08/294478/index.htm.

iv   Conor McQuiston, "How Often Do NFL Free Agents Actually Finish Out Their Contracts?," Pro Football Focus, March 18, 2022, https://www.pff.com/news/nfl-free-agents-finish-out-contracts.

v   "NFL's Richest Contract Goes to Bledsoe," *New York Times*, March 8, 2001, https://www.nytimes.com/2001/03/08/sports/plus-nfl-richest-contract-goes-to-bledsoe.html.

ABOUT THE AUTHOR

Robert Glazer is the Founder and Chairman of the Board of global partnership marketing agency Acceleration Partners. He was also the co-founder and chairman of BrandCycle, which was sold to Stack Commerce/TPG in 2021. A serial entrepreneur and award-winning executive, Bob has a passion for helping individuals and organizations build their capacity and elevate their performance.

Under Bob's leadership, Acceleration Partners became a recognized global leader in the affiliate and partner marketing industry. Acceleration Partners has received numerous industry and company culture awards, including Glassdoor's Employees' Choice Awards, *Ad Age*'s Best Place to Work, *Entrepreneur*'s Top Company Culture, *Inc.*'s Best Place to Work, Great Place to

Work and *Fortune*'s Best Small & Medium Workplaces, *Digiday*'s Most Committed to Work-Life Balance, and *Boston Globe*'s Top Workplaces.

Bob was named to Glassdoor's list of Top CEOs of Small and Medium Companies in the US twice, ranking as high as #2.

Bob shares his ideas and insights via Friday Forward, a popular weekly inspirational newsletter that reaches over 200,000 individuals and business leaders across sixty-plus countries. He is a #1 *Wall Street Journal, USA Today,* and international bestselling author of six books including *Elevate, Friday Forward, Moving to Outcomes,* and *How to Make Virtual Teams Work.* He is also the host of the Elevate Podcast, a top podcast for entrepreneurship in over twenty countries with over one million downloads.

Bob's writing reaches over five million people around the globe each year who resonate with his topics, which range from partner marketing and entrepreneurship to company culture, capacity building, remote work, and leadership. His work has been featured in *Harvard Business Review, The Today Show, Business Insider, Fast Company, Inc., Forbes,* and *Entrepreneur.* He also speaks globally to companies and organizations on themes related to business growth, culture, building capacity, and performance, and has spoken on the TEDx stage.

A strong believer in giving back, Bob serves on the Board of Directors for BUILD Boston, is a member of the Global Council for Junior Achievement Worldwide, served as a global leader in Entrepreneurs' Organization (EO), and founded The Fifth Night charitable event.

Outside of work, Bob can likely be found skiing, cycling, reading, traveling, spending quality time with his family, or overseeing some sort of home renovation project.

Learn more about Bob at **robertglazer.com.**

ADDITIONAL RESOURCES:

To learn more about the tools and processes described in this book, I encourage you to explore our resources page, available at **robertglazer.com/eyt-resources**. This page has a list of resources that is updated regularly.

I am always interested in new ideas, partnerships, and feedback and would love to hear from you. Feel free to drop a line at elevate@robertglazer.com. I work to read every email and respond to most.

MORE ABOUT ME:

To learn more about me, my writing, or speaking and partnerships opportunities, please visit **robertglazer.com.**

ABOUT MY COMPANY:

accelerationpartners.com

COURSES

To learn how to better apply the lessons I write about to your life and career, check out my on-demand courses. In particular, I recommend you check out my course on Discovering and Developing Core Values, which was discussed in detail in this book.

Core Values Course: **corevaluescourse.com**

All Courses: **robertglazer.com/courses**

THE ELEVATE PODCAST

Hear in-depth conversations with the world's top CEOs, authors, thinkers, and performers, including many of the thought leaders mentioned in this book! **robertglazer.com/podcast**

ALSO BY ROBERT GLAZER

If you enjoyed this book, I invite you to check out my *Wall Street Journal* and *USA Today* bestsellers *Elevate: Push Beyond Your Limits and Unlock Success in Yourself and Others* and *How to Thrive in the Virtual Workplace*, as well as *Friday Forward: Inspiration & Motivation to End Your Week Stronger Than It Started* and *Moving to Outcomes: Why Partnerships are the Future of Marketing*. Learn more at:

Elevate: **robertglazer.com/elevate**

How to Thrive in the Virtual Workplace:

robertglazer.com/thrive

Friday Forward: **fridayforwardbook.com**

Moving to Outcomes: **robertglazer.com/outcomes**

PLEASE LEAVE A REVIEW

If you got value out of *Elevate Your Team,* I'd love if you could leave a rating and review on your favorite bookseller website. This is the best way to help other people discover the book, so I would appreciate your review: **robertglazer.com/review**